Get Out of Debt Fast

The Strategic, Proven Roadmap to Rebuild Your Finances, Reclaim Your Peace, and Achieve Lasting Financial Freedom
—Without Stress

"Debt is not the end of your story—it's just a chapter. Starting today, you hold the pen, and the next pages are all about freedom."

rg.
REGINE GODEFROY
AUTHOR

📃 Copyright

Get Out of Debt Fast: Strategic, Proven Roadmap to Rebuild Your Finances, Reclaim Your Peace, and Achieve Lasting Financial Freedom—Without Stress

Published by Shopunlocked LLC

ISBN: 978-1-968744-14-4

Printed in the United States of America
First Edition, 2025

To request permission, contact:
📧 support@shopunlocked.com
🌐 www.shopunlocked.com

This page is left intentionally blank

TABLE OF CONTENTS

◇ PART 1 – LEARN IT

◇ PART 2 – DO IT

This page is left intentionally blank

PREFACE

> **This is the book i wish someone had handed me a few years ago.**

Let's be honest for a second.

Most people don't get into debt because they're dumb.

They get into debt because they're doing what they were told:
Go to school. Get the car. Help your family.
Swipe the card for groceries.
Take the "0% interest" offer because you need that emergency dental work.
Say yes to your kid's birthday party even if rent is due next week.

Debt doesn't always come from irresponsibility.
It comes from trying to *live.*
From trying to *survive.*
From trying to *keep your dignity intact* while holding everything together.

But the shame?
Oh, the shame sticks around like it was invited.

You avoid checking your bank app.
You stay silent when your partner asks, "Did you pay that bill yet?"

You nod along when people talk about investing... but inside, you're wondering how to keep the lights on.

And worst of all?

You feel like this is **your fault**.
Like you must've messed up somewhere.
Like you're not "good with money."
Like everyone else knows something you don't.

Let me tell you the truth:

You are not the problem. The system was built to keep you confused, busy, and in just enough debt to never really get free.

They want you focused on your minimum payment.
They want you addicted to the reward points.
They want you too tired to question the fine print.

Because when you're in debt, you're profitable—to them.

But this book?

This book is about flipping the script.

This book is your permission slip to stop feeling ashamed and start feeling **powerful**.

It's not just about getting out of debt—it's about getting your life back.

It's about facing the numbers without the panic.
It's about forgiving yourself for the past and building new habits for the future.
It's about making decisions like someone who's in control again—because you will be.

Inside these pages, we will walk you through it all:

- The emotional traps.

- The interest math.
- The habits that are quietly draining you.
- The blueprint that works even if you've failed before.

We won't just tell you to "budget better."
We'll show you how.
We won't just preach discipline.
We'll help you feel *safe* enough to build it.

This book is for the person who's tired of pretending.
Tired of hiding.
Tired of working hard and still feeling stuck.
Tired of seeing money disappear as fast as it comes in.

If that's you...

You're exactly where you need to be.

Not because everything is perfect.
But because **you're finally ready to do something about it**.

You don't need more motivation. You need a system—and a little bit of fire.
This book is both.

Turn the page.
Let's light it up.

— Regine

◇ PART 1 – LEARN IT

What they never teach you about debt

> *"Debt may have slowed you down, but it has not broken you. The road ahead is yours to claim."*

CHAPTER 1

Debt and the Heavy Silence We Carry

☑ 1.1– The shame no one talks about

> *"I used to avoid the mailbox. Every envelope felt like a small panic attack."*

Debt shame runs deep—not because of the number, but because of the **story our brain connects to that number.**

🔄 Rewire Your Story

Shame around money often starts early—being told you "wasted money," "should've known better," or watched parents panic over bills. Your brain linked *debt = bad person* instead of *debt = bad system or lack of tools.*

These beliefs aren't permanent—they're wired from emotion, not fact.

Today, you can tell your brain a new truth:

> *"I have debt, but I am not broken.*
>
> *I am learning.*

> *I am capable.*
> *I am healing this story."*

Every time you face your numbers with compassion, you're reprocessing and rewiring that shame into strength. No judgment, keep reading ...

✦Meet Nadia✦

She's a home health aide and single mother of two. She works hard, takes care of her kids, and always makes sure there's food on the table—even if that means skipping meals herself. She doesn't shop for herself, doesn't go on vacations, and hasn't had a new pair of shoes in two years.

And yet, her **credit card balance is still rising.**

She doesn't tell anyone. Not her sisters. Not her best friend. Not even her oldest daughter, who once asked, "Mom, why are you always worried after opening the mail?"

Nadia isn't irresponsible. She's exhausted, overworked, and overwhelmed. Her debt is not from shopping sprees—it's from **emergencies, late fees, school clothes, and rent gaps.** She's ashamed of it anyway.

This is the silent pain so many of us carry.

Debt isn't just a financial number—it's an emotional weight.

We avoid opening our bank apps.

We feel judged—even if it's only by our own reflection.

We make minimum payments and pray we'll feel better next month.

But we don't.

And over time, avoidance **feeds the debt** ✦

🔍 1.2– Why Facing Debt Is an Act of Power

If you're reading this book, you've already made your **first bold move**.

That alone makes you stronger than the version of you who kept looking away.

You didn't pick up this book by accident. You did it because something in you is **ready to stop running**.

Here's something they never told us in school:

Debt is not a character flaw—it's a financial wound.
And wounds need care, not shame.

You are not lazy. You are not broken.
You are simply trying to survive with the tools you were given.
Now we're going to build better ones.

Facing your debt doesn't mean you failed.
It means you've decided **you deserve better** than living in fear.

You might feel like facing your debt confirms your failure.
In fact, the opposite is true—**it proves you're ready to change.**

🔄 Rewire Your Story

Avoidance is a brain-based survival mechanism. If your nervous system learned that facing money leads to fear or judgment, it naturally protected you by ignoring it. This isn't laziness—it's **emotional defense**.

Healing begins when we revisit those moments with new safety.

Tell yourself:

> *"I'm safe now.*
>
> *I have tools I didn't have before.*
>
> *I can look at my debt and not freeze."*

This is you forming a new neural path where courage replaces fear, clarity replaces panic.

💬 1.3– Don't Let Fear Steal Your Freedom

Fear is the body's way of staying alert—but when it becomes chronic, it paralyzes progress. You are not meant to live in fear.

🔄 Rewire Your Story

If money fear is always in the background—when spending, opening apps, or checking mail—it's likely tied to an old experience: financial instability, family pressure, or loss.

Your brain stored that fear to "keep you safe." But you're not in that same moment anymore.

Now you get to install this new truth:

> *"I am doing something different this time. My fear is a signal, not a stop sign."*

Each time you pause, breathe, and choose progress over panic, you rewire safety into your financial journey.

Here are a few truths to hold onto when it feels hard to keep going:

✦ *"You are not your bank balance. You are your choices moving forward."*

✦ *"Debt is loud. But your commitment to change is louder."*

✦ *"You can't fix what you don't face—but you don't have to face it alone."*

✦ *"Real strength is choosing to stay in the fight even when the numbers scare you."*

When you get overwhelmed, come back to these.
Stick them on your mirror. Make one your phone wallpaper.

You're not just reading a book—you're building a better life.

🧠 1.4– What This Book Will—and Won't—Do

It's important that you know this journey is not about pressure, perfection, or pretending it's easy.

🔄 Rewire Your Story

If you've failed at past debt plans or financial "fixes," your brain might expect failure again. It's guarding your heart.

Failure narratives can become embedded like emotional scars.

Let's soften that:

> *"That was then. This is now. I'm not repeating—I'm rebuilding."*

By reading this, you're already showing your nervous system that learning can be safe, kind, and doable. That's progress.

Let's set expectations now.

✅ What this book *will* do:

- Explain debt and money in **plain language**
- Give you **real-life stories** and relatable examples
- Offer **step-by-step tools** to build your own plan
- Walk beside you without judgment

🚫 What this book *won't* do:

- Use complicated finance terms to confuse you
- Assume one method fits everyone
- Promise "instant debt-free" miracles

This journey is **yours**. You'll win using the strategy that fits your life, not someone else's formula.

▧ SELF-CHECK: Face the Debt Wall

Now let's begin the most important part of section 1: **telling yourself the truth—gently.**

You might hesitate to write your numbers down. That's normal. It feels like putting emotional wounds onto paper.

We're not calculating anything yet. We're just starting the conversation.

🧩 Exercise: Face the Debt Wall

Purpose:
Break the silence and fear. Start listing all your debts honestly, without judgment.

When:
Right now—before you move on.

Steps:

1. Write down every debt you know you have.

- Credit card, car loan, student loan, mortgage, personal loan, etc.

2. Note the **total balance**, **interest rate** (if you know it), **monthly payment**, and **how long you've had it**.
3. Leave extra space—you'll add more details later.

This list will grow as you understand more. Think of it as your **financial map.**

📝 Worksheet

Use a notebook or write directly here:

Debt Type	Amount	Interest Rate	Minimum Payment	Years in Debt

📌 *Just write what you know. No shame. No stress. This is the beginning of your breakthrough.*

- Type of debt (student loan, credit card, car loan, etc.)
- Who you owe
- Total balance
- Interest rate (if you know it)
- Monthly payment
- How long you've been in debt

📌 *This list will grow. You'll come back to it often, like a map. For now, just write honestly.*

🗒 Hands-On Example

Debt Type	Amount	Interest (Yearly)	Min Payment	Years in Debt
Credit Card	$5,200	24.99%	$160	3 years
Car Loan	$9,000	7.5%	$280	2 years

🔄 Rewire Your Story

If listing your debts brings a lump in your throat or a knot in your stomach, pause and honor that.
That's your brain surfacing stored emotion—and that's okay.

Use this exercise not to judge yourself, but to begin a new pattern:

> *"I am allowed to look without punishing myself.*
> *I am allowed to begin without having it all figured out."*

Writing your debt is not just math—it's a reclaiming. Each number you write down is a **neural link breaking free from shame.**

📲 Ready to assess your financial foundation?

👉 Take this Quiz : Building a Strong Financial Foundation

Purpose:

Test your understanding of budgeting basics, debt-to-income ratio, financial health, income types, and expense categories (fixed vs. variable).

Topics:

- Budgeting purpose and components
- Debt-to-income ratio
- Financial health evaluation
- Income definitions
- Fixed vs. variable expenses

📌 Chapter Summary: What You've Conquered

You've made it through the hardest part: beginning.

Let's pause and recognize what you now understand—because awareness is the first step to freedom.

- ☑ **You now know why it's so hard to face your numbers.**
  Avoiding your bank balance isn't laziness—it's emotional self-protection.
- ☑ **You've acknowledged that shame thrives in silence.**
  Many of us hide debt from loved ones, thinking we're the only ones struggling. We're not.
- ☑ **You've seen how shame leads to avoidance, and avoidance leads to deeper debt.**
  The cycle isn't your fault—but now, you've begun to break it.
- ☑ **You've claimed your first win.**
  Picking up this book, reading this chapter—that's already an act of courage.
- ☑ **You've learned that debt is not a character flaw.**
  It's a financial wound, and wounds can heal with the right care and strategy.
- ☑ **You understand that facing your debt is an act of power.**
  Looking at your numbers, naming your fear, and deciding to change—that's how peace begins.

- ☑ **You've begun telling yourself a new story.** One where your past doesn't define your next move. Where discipline replaces panic. Where freedom is no longer a fantasy—it's a plan.

📖 *Now take a breath, look at your list, and remind yourself: I've already started.*

✹ Next Step

Before we move forward, take a moment to acknowledge what you've just done. You've broken the silence. You've looked at your reality with courage instead of fear. That's no small thing.

But now comes an important question: *How did we get here in the first place?* What patterns, systems, and silent messages led so many good, hardworking people into debt without even realizing it?

In Chapter 2, we'll explore those answers with honesty and compassion—so you can stop blaming yourself and start understanding what really happened.

This page is left intentionally blank

CHAPTER 2

How We Fall In (And Why It's Not Your Fault)

◇ 2.1– Society Is Built on Borrowing

It's not your imagination—it really is harder to stay out of debt today than it was for our parents or grandparents. In almost every direction we look, borrowing is normalized. You're told to finance your education, lease your car, swipe your card for everyday purchases, and "build credit" before you even understand what credit means. Every commercial whisper the same message: *"If you want it, buy it now. Pay later."*

We live in a system designed for us to borrow. Wages haven't kept up with the rising cost of living, and access to quick credit is easier than access to trustworthy financial education. We're handed credit cards before we're taught how interest works. This isn't just a money issue—it's a structural one. And it's not your fault.

Rewire Your Story

When we see phrases like "0% for 6 months" or "Buy now, pay later," our brain hears: *"This is free. This is safe. This is smart."* But what we often miss is the **math** behind it.

Let's say you finance a $600 couch with a 0% promotion. You're required to pay it off in 6 months—or else a 29.99% interest rate kicks in retroactively from day one. If you miss just one payment or delay, you now owe nearly $800. Not so cheap anymore.

Same with store financing: a phone on layaway may seem manageable at $25/month, but if you stretch it over 24 months with added service fees, you've paid double.

If you've internalized guilt for "falling into the trap," know this: your nervous system may have learned early on that short-term comfort was safer than long-term uncertainty. Tell yourself:

> *"I did the best I could with what I had. Now I do the math first."*

◇ 2.2– We Were Never Taught

If you graduated from high school without knowing how a credit score works, how to calculate interest, or how to budget, you're not alone. Most schools still don't teach basic personal finance. Meanwhile, families often avoid the topic out of fear, shame, or lack of knowledge themselves.

Let's break some of those phrases down:

- **"Finance your car"** means taking a loan to pay for a car over time. It sounds convenient, but if the interest rate is high or the loan term is long, you could pay $30,000 for a $20,000 vehicle—and still owe more than it's worth years later.
- **"Lease a car"** means you're renting the car long-term. Monthly payments may be lower, but at the end you own nothing (you don't own the car). You've paid for temporary use without building any value.
- **"Finance your education"** means taking out student loans. In the U.S., the average borrower owes $37,000 or more in student loans. Education can be powerful—but if you choose a degree with low earning potential and high cost, it can trap you.
- **"Get a credit card"** often sounds like freedom. But every swipe comes with invisible interest unless you pay the full balance monthly. Most people don't—and over time, balances snowball.
- **"Buy now, pay later"** may work for small purchases if paid on time, but missing payments means fees, credit damage, and future limits. It's not a gift. It's a delayed bill.
- **"Inflation"** means your money loses value over time. A $100 grocery run in 2019 may cost $130 today. If your income doesn't grow with inflation, you slowly fall behind.

🔄 Rewire Your Story

Instead of replaying the story of "I should have known better," shift it to:

> *"I'm not late—I'm right on time to learn what matters now."*

Every chapter you read, every insight you gain is a message to your brain:

> *"This time, I lead with knowledge."*

◇ 2.3– Why Good People End Up in Debt

Debt isn't a moral failure. It's often the outcome of good intentions, emergencies, and pressure to provide. Maybe you wanted your kids to feel normal at school. Maybe you had a medical issue. Maybe you just didn't know any better. All of those are human experiences—not evidence of irresponsibility.

But there's another trap—**living beyond your means without realizing it.** It starts small: a better phone, a nicer apartment, a birthday splurge. You convince yourself, *"It's normal. Everyone around me does it."* And if you grew up in a home with a certain lifestyle, there may be a part of you that believes *"downgrading"* is failure.

Over time, the brain forms a belief: *"I have to keep up, even if it hurts."* And that's when the damage grows silently.

Wake-Up Exercise

Ask yourself:

What story am I trying to prove with my lifestyle?

Am I living for comfort—or for appearances?

If your bank account could talk, would it say you're being honest about your capacity?

Try this:

Write down the **three most expensive lifestyle habits** you maintain today (car, apartment, phone, dining, etc.). For each, ask:

- Did I choose this out of true need or emotional habit?
- Would I be embarrassed to downgrade it? Why?
- What's the actual monthly cost vs. what I gain emotionally?

Lifestyle habit 1:

___

___

___

Lifestyle habit 2:

___

___

___

Lifestyle habit 3:

____

____

____

Rewire Your Story

Tell yourself:

> *"I don't need to prove anything to anyone. My value isn't tied to image. Real freedom is having choices—not just looking like I do."*

◇ 2.4– The "Emergency to Emergency" Trap

Living paycheck to paycheck is not just exhausting—it's traumatic. When you don't have a cushion, every flat tire, doctor visit, or unexpected bill becomes a crisis. So what happens? You borrow. Again and again.

This cycle teaches your brain that money is temporary and that survival is luck. Over time, it wires in the belief that you'll never "get ahead."

But here's the truth: **You can break the cycle.** And it starts with understanding the foundations.

If you haven't read "***Start With This***" *the book released before this one*, now is the time. It covers:

- How to build a practical budget using the 50/30/20 rule
- Why saving comes before paying off debt

- How to separate needs from wants
- The importance of tracking your income and expenses
- How to set realistic savings goals—even when you feel behind

This debt elimination book builds directly on those principles. If budgeting still feels confusing, pause now and revisit "**Start With This**" *by the same author* **Regine Godefroy**. It will help you move forward here with confidence.	**Scan book here**

Rewire Your Story

Instead of believing *"There's never enough,"* shift to:

> *"I have the tools now to begin. My money story is being rewritten with every choice I make."*

◇ 2.5– Buying Peace of Mind on Credit

Sometimes we buy not because we want something, but because we want relief. Buying gives us a sense of control—even if it's just for a moment.

That feeling is real. But the cost is also real.

Let's talk about gratification—the emotional payoff of a purchase.

Unhealthy gratification happens when we spend to numb discomfort. It feels good for 30 minutes... then the guilt sets in.

Healthy gratification comes from saving, delaying, planning. It feels boring at first—but gives lasting peace, not financial regret.

So when you say, "I deserve this," ask: Do I deserve 10 minutes of escape—or 10 months of control?

🔄 Rewire Your Story

Acknowledge the emotional root: *"I was looking for peace, not products. I needed relief, not more debt."* Begin practicing self-care that doesn't require spending. Every time you pause and choose differently, you are reprogramming your nervous system to find peace within control, not consumption. Remind yourself:

> *"Discipline is a form of self-love. My peace will come from power, not purchases."*

◇ 2.6– Giving while drowning: the hidden cost of generosity

Let's talk about generosity—the kind that's celebrated, praised, and sometimes... dangerous

🔎 **Real-Life Case:** Giving Away Cash While Carrying a Mortgage and Credit Card

✦Tania is a warm-hearted woman who owns a small property she rents out for $1,500/month. She also works part-time and has decent income.
She's generous with her money—helps friends, sends remittances, and loves hosting family dinners.

But she only pays the **minimum** on her mortgage and credit cards every month. Total debts:

- Mortgage balance: $110,000 @ 6.5%
- Credit card: $5,200 @ 24.99%

Her monthly credit card payment is around $160. She once spent $2,000 helping a friend in need, while still carrying a 25% credit card balance. Her thinking?

"It's just a small payment every month, and I'm doing good."

Here's the truth:

- She's being charged over $1,200/year in credit card interest.
- She's stretching her mortgage to 30 years and giving away **tens of thousands** to the bank.
- She thinks she's helping, but her future self will be in more debt, with fewer options.

> *Giving generously is beautiful—but not if it keeps you in chains.*

Let's explore why we give:

- Some give to **feel useful**, especially when their self-worth is tied to being needed.
- Others give to **avoid guilt**—saying yes out of fear of being called selfish.
- Some give for **recognition or validation**—even unconsciously.
- Some believe **sacrifice equals love**—even when it depletes them.

And finally, some give because it's all they've ever seen modeled—generosity as a way to belong, to feel noble, or to cope with their own scarcity trauma.

Here's the truth: **You can still be generous. But from a full cup.**

> 💡 *"You can't pour from an empty cup. Pay off the chains first. Help others from a place of strength."*

🔄 Rewire Your Story

Tell yourself:

> *"True generosity flows from strength. I protect my future so I can give even more later—with joy, not resentment."*

Investing in Dreams Without Math

Creative energy and emotional excitement can lead to financial blindness.

This following case should be very relatable to creators, artists, musicians, and unexperienced entrepreneurs who lead with passion but often ignore the math.

🔎 Real-Life Case: The Artist's Debt Trap – Dream walking into the Red

✦Marcus is a talented musician. His energy is contagious, and he has a big heart.
He believes in his gift so much that he borrows money—credit cards, personal loans, even borrowing from friends—to organize events that he's *sure* will be a hit.

He sees the launch in his mind like a movie: big crowd, long line, great music, full bar, merch flying off the table. So he starts spending—on sound, lighting, flyers, outfits, transport, team, rentals.

But here's the math after the show:

- Door revenue: $2,100
- Bar share: $0 (venue kept it)
- Expenses: $4,300
- RED Balance: –$2,200

Marcus shrugs it off.

"It's an *investment*. Next time I'll do better."

But he does it again. And again. He starts putting $50 here, $100 there on different cards. It becomes normal to be $8,000–$10,000 in debt "for the dream."

👉 **Reality check:**

If you're consistently losing money, it's not an investment—it's **gambling on hope**.

> 💡 *"Using your creative brain is beautiful, but not if it makes you ignore the numbers. That's not dreaming. That's blindfolding."*

🧾 Self-Check: The "Dream vs. Math" Test

Purpose: Help creatives/artists check the numbers behind events or launches.

Steps:

1. Write down all the expected income from a project (tickets, sales, tips).
2. Write down all the actual costs (before/during/after).
3. Compare: income – expenses.
4. Write a reflection: Was this a profit, a loss, or a donation to the dream?

Worksheet

Income from Project	Amount
Regular Tickets	
VIP Tickets	
Consumables	
Tips	
Sponsor 1	
Sponsor 2	

Expense from Project	Amount
Band transportation	
Lead transportation	
Logistics & Per Diem Band	
Clothing	
Press / Influencers	
Flyers	

Hands-on Example:

- Income: \$2,100 (door) + \$0 (bar) = \$2,100
- Expenses: \$1,500 (logistics) + \$800 (staff) = \$2,300
- Result: –\$200

- Reflection: "I thought I'd earn, but didn't check the bar contract. Lesson: don't spend before confirming income."

◇ 2.7– Personal Reflection Prompt:

Think of one moment when you felt overwhelmed by money.

- What did you do?
- How did it make you feel?"
- What would you want your future self to do differently?

🧠 2.8– The Inner Dialogue Check-In:

Take a deep breath. Now ask:

> *What does your inner voice say about your money today? If it's cruel, is it helping?*

Does it say:

- "I'm irresponsible."
- "I'll never get out of this."
- "I'm behind. I'm ashamed. I should know better."

Or could it say something new:

- "I've learned so much already."

- "I'm healing the patterns I was never taught to question."
- "I'm doing better than I was yesterday."

You're allowed to talk to yourself with the same compassion you give to others. In fact, it's necessary.

Let this be the voice you install:

> *"I am not my past mistakes. I am my next smart choice."*

📌 Chapter Summary: What You've Conquered

You didn't fall because you were weak. You fell because no one showed you the ledges. Now you see them. Now you climb.

- **Why "buy now, pay later" feels safe—but usually isn't.** These offers are marketed as harmless convenience, but they often come with traps that cost you more in the long run.
- **You're not broken—you were never taught.** Most people never learned how credit, loans, or interest work. Now you're learning with fresh eyes.
- **How well-meaning choices (helping others, chasing dreams) often lead to silent debt.** Kindness and ambition aren't the problem—a lack of planning is. The solution is awareness and balance.
- **The difference between emotional spending and true gratification.** One brings guilt, the other builds peace. Knowing which is which can change everything.

- **The importance of catching yourself when living beyond your means feels normal.** Lifestyle inflation and social pressure can fool even the most careful of us.
- **Why living paycheck to paycheck isn't just hard—it's a system you can escape.** There are real steps to break the cycle and reclaim your peace.
- **Society profits when we stay in debt.** You weren't targeted because you were weak. You were targeted because you were human.
- **Emotional spending is understandable, but unsustainable.** It's not about blame—it's about finding healthier ways to soothe and restore.
- **Generosity is powerful, but you must protect your own oxygen mask first.** Giving from a place of strength means you can give more—without breaking yourself.
- **Real change starts by telling the truth with compassion.** This chapter helped you begin that truth. And you're still here. That's progress.

Get ready for Chapter 3, where we dive into how debt works mathematically, how interest **quietly steals your future**, and how you can reclaim control.

CHAPTER 3

The Real Cost of Debt

The Math and the Mind Games

L*ogic and financial mechanics*: It's where they begin to see the trap: interest, amortization, revolving debt.

Many people in debt have never fully understood **how** it all works.

Once they "get the math," they stop blaming themselves so much. This primes them for deeper emotional reflection.

3.1– How Debt Keeps You Broke (Without You Noticing)

Nadia thought she was being responsible. She paid her credit card every month—never skipped. But she never looked closely at her statement. Three years later, her balance had barely budged.

She felt stuck. Angry. Embarrassed. *"I've been paying faithfully... how do I still owe the same?"*

Here's why: most of her payment was going to **interest**, not her actual balance. It's the trap that keeps millions of people in debt year after year.

Credit cards and personal loans are designed so that minimum payments mostly cover interest—keeping your balance alive, while slowly draining your income.

If you only pay the $105 minimum on a $5,000 balance at 24.99%, it will take approximately **233 months** to pay off... Total interest you will pay: $19,389.31

Total to pay back: $24,389.31

This is how debt keeps you broke: by giving you the illusion of progress while your wealth leaks away.

🔄 Rewire Your Story

If you've ever thought, *"I'm doing what I can, but nothing changes,"* remember this: it's not your math that's broken—it's the system. Your nervous system may have learned to celebrate small payments without knowing they weren't actually helping.

Tell yourself:

> *"Now I understand the trap. Now I move with clarity, not just effort."*

Let's take an example on a $5,000 personal loan at 26.99% APR. This loan is to be paid off in 5 years. Start date August 2025.

Summary of the REAL outcome:

Monthly payment **$152.65**	Total interest paid **$4,158.81**
Number of payments **60**	Total to be repaid **$9,158.81**
Estimated payoff **August 2030**	Effective annual % **30.59%**

Here the detail of what really happens while you are making regular payments:

From year 2025 to 2028, most of your payments go towards interest (It has been front loaded – in other words, the bank is getting its money back FIRST). From 2028 to 2030, most of your payments go towards the capital (the amount owed in the first place)

Year	Payment	Principal	Interest	Balance
Aug 2025	-	-	-	$5,000.00
2025	$610.60	$166.26	$444.33	$4,833.74
2026	$1,831.80	$597.49	$1,234.27	$4,236.25
2027	$1,831.80	$780.27	$1,051.49	$3,455.98
2028	$1,831.80	$1,018.98	$812.78	$2,437.00
2029	$1,831.80	$1,330.70	$501.06	$1,106.30
2030	$1,221.20	$1,106.30	$114.88	$0.00
Final total	$9,158.81	$5,000.00	$4,158.81	$0.00

🔎 How Interest Eats Away Your Income

Interest is essentially the "rent" you pay to use someone else's money. Every month you carry a balance on a loan or credit card, a percentage of that balance is added as interest. This payment doesn't reduce your debt—it's simply a cost for borrowing.

If you owe $5,000 at 24% APR, you're paying about $100 a month in interest alone. That's $1,200 a year that could have gone toward groceries, savings, or paying down the actual debt. The more you owe, and the higher the interest rate, the bigger the bite from your income. Over time, these small bites add up to huge amounts of money spent on nothing but the privilege of owing money.

> *High-interest debt means you're working hard to enrich the lender instead of building your own wealth.*

🔎 Explaining Minimum Payments

A minimum payment is the smallest amount your lender will accept to keep your account in good standing. It's designed to protect the lender, not to help you get out of debt quickly.

Credit cards often set the minimum as:

A flat percentage of your balance (e.g., 2%–4%) or

Interest for the month + 1% of your principal

On a $5,000 balance at 24.99% APR, the minimum could be around $100–$150. Pay only the minimum, and most of that money will go toward interest, with just a tiny fraction reducing the actual balance. As a result, it can take years—even decades—to pay off the debt, and you'll pay back several times what you borrowed.

> *Minimum payments keep you afloat but don't move you toward shore.*

🔎 Interest Compounding Quietly

Compounding is when interest is charged not just on your original balance, but also on any unpaid interest from previous months. This is why debt can feel like it's growing even if you're making payments.

Here's how it works:

Month 1: You owe $5,000. Interest at 2% adds $100. New balance = $5,100.

Month 2: Interest is calculated on $5,100, not just the original $5,000. That adds $102, pushing the balance higher.

This repeats every month—interest on top of interest.

Because it happens quietly in the background, you may not notice how much it's costing you until the balance has ballooned.

> *Compounding can work in your favor with savings, but it's your enemy in debt.*

3.2– What Is Amortization?

Let's say you take out a $20,000 car loan at 7% interest for 5 years. The dealer tells you the monthly payment is $396. You think: *"I can handle that."*

But here's the truth: in the first year, most of that $396 is going to **interest**, not the actual car loan. You won't really start attacking the principal until year 2 or 3.

This system is called **amortization**—a structure where your payments are the same every month, but the breakdown between interest and principal **shifts slowly** over time.

It makes the loan *look manageable*, but delays your actual progress.

This is why your loan statement can be shocking. You paid thousands—and yet the balance barely moved.

Here is a visual recap starting August 2025 for example:

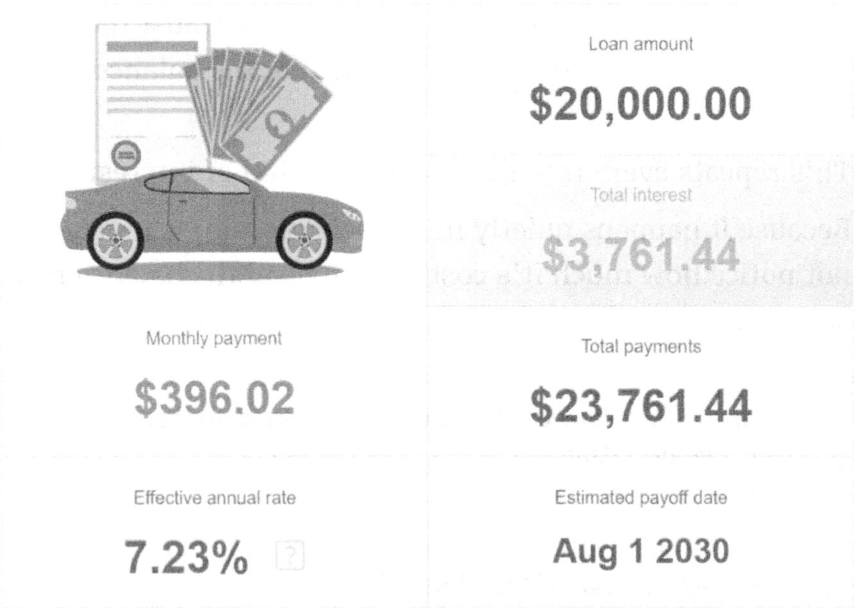

Car Loan Repayments by Month

Payment date	Payment	Principal	Interest	Balance
Aug 2025	-	-	-	$20,000.00
Sep 2025	$396.02	$279.36	$116.67	$19,720.64
Oct 2025	$396.02	$280.99	$115.04	$19,439.66
Nov 2025	$396.02	$282.63	$113.40	$19,157.03
Dec 2025	$396.02	$284.27	$111.75	$18,872.76
2025	**$1,584.10**	**$1,127.24**	**$456.85**	**$18,872.76**
Jan 2026	$396.02	$285.93	$110.09	$18,586.82
Feb 2026	$396.02	$287.60	$108.42	$18,299.22
Mar 2026	$396.02	$289.28	$106.75	$18,009.94
Apr 2026	$396.02	$290.97	$105.06	$17,718.98
May 2026	$396.02	$292.66	$103.36	$17,426.31
Jun 2026	$396.02	$294.37	$101.65	$17,131.94
Jul 2026	$396.02	$296.09	$99.94	$16,835.86
Aug 2026	$396.02	$297.81	$98.21	$16,538.04
Sep 2026	$396.02	$299.55	$96.47	$16,238.49
Oct 2026	$396.02	$301.30	$94.72	$15,937.19
Nov 2026	$396.02	$303.06	$92.97	$15,634.13
Dec 2026	$396.02	$304.82	$91.20	$15,329.31
2026	**$4,752.29**	**$3,543.45**	**$1,208.84**	**$15,329.31**
Jan 2027	$396.02	$306.60	$89.42	$15,022.70
Feb 2027	$396.02	$308.39	$87.63	$14,714.31
Mar 2027	$396.02	$310.19	$85.83	$14,404.12
Apr 2027	$396.02	$312.00	$84.02	$14,092.12
May 2027	$396.02	$313.82	$82.20	$13,778.30
Jun 2027	$396.02	$315.65	$80.37	$13,462.65
Jul 2027	$396.02	$317.49	$78.53	$13,145.16
Aug 2027	$396.02	$319.34	$76.68	$12,825.82
Sep 2027	$396.02	$321.21	$74.82	$12,504.61
Oct 2027	$396.02	$323.08	$72.94	$12,181.53
Nov 2027	$396.02	$324.97	$71.06	$11,856.56
Dec 2027	$396.02	$326.86	$69.16	$11,529.70

2027	**$4,752.29**	**$3,799.60**	**$952.68**	**$11,529.70**
Jan 2028	$396.02	$328.77	$67.26	$11,200.94
Feb 2028	$396.02	$330.69	$65.34	$10,870.25
Mar 2028	$396.02	$332.61	$63.41	$10,537.64
Apr 2028	$396.02	$334.55	$61.47	$10,203.08
May 2028	$396.02	$336.51	$59.52	$9,866.58
Jun 2028	$396.02	$338.47	$57.56	$9,528.11
Jul 2028	$396.02	$340.44	$55.58	$9,187.66
Aug 2028	$396.02	$342.43	$53.59	$8,845.23
Sep 2028	$396.02	$344.43	$51.60	$8,500.81
Oct 2028	$396.02	$346.44	$49.59	$8,154.37
Nov 2028	$396.02	$348.46	$47.57	$7,805.92
Dec 2028	$396.02	$350.49	$45.53	$7,455.43
2028	**$4,752.29**	**$4,074.28**	**$678.01**	**$7,455.43**
Jan 2029	$396.02	$352.53	$43.49	$7,102.89
Feb 2029	$396.02	$354.59	$41.43	$6,748.30
Mar 2029	$396.02	$356.66	$39.37	$6,391.64
Apr 2029	$396.02	$358.74	$37.28	$6,032.90
May 2029	$396.02	$360.83	$35.19	$5,672.07
Jun 2029	$396.02	$362.94	$33.09	$5,309.13
Jul 2029	$396.02	$365.05	$30.97	$4,944.08
Aug 2029	$396.02	$367.18	$28.84	$4,576.90
Sep 2029	$396.02	$369.33	$26.70	$4,207.57
Oct 2029	$396.02	$371.48	$24.54	$3,836.09
Nov 2029	$396.02	$373.65	$22.38	$3,462.44
Dec 2029	$396.02	$375.83	$20.20	$3,086.62
2029	**$4,752.29**	**$4,368.81**	**$383.48**	**$3,086.62**
Jan 2030	$396.02	$378.02	$18.01	$2,708.60
Feb 2030	$396.02	$380.22	$15.80	$2,328.38
Mar 2030	$396.02	$382.44	$13.58	$1,945.93
Apr 2030	$396.02	$384.67	$11.35	$1,561.26
May 2030	$396.02	$386.92	$9.11	$1,174.34
Jun 2030	$396.02	$389.17	$6.85	$785.17
Jul 2030	$396.02	$391.44	$4.58	$393.73
Aug 2030	$396.02	$393.73	$2.30	$0.00

Now imagine this system across mortgages, student loans, personal loans. It's not a coincidence. It's a model designed to maximize profit.

Banks win when you pay slowly.

🔧 Mini Math Example

- $20,000 loan @ 7% over 60 months
- Total paid: $23,761.44
- Interest paid: $3,761.44
- True cost = almost 19% more than sticker price
- Amortized loans, minimum payments, and daily interest
- Visual example of a 5-year loan breakdown
- Why equal payments don't mean equal progress

3.3– Credit Cards vs. Loans vs. Lines of Credit

- Revolving vs. installment debt explained
- How they work
- Which one traps you faster

Not all debt works the same. To take back control, you need to understand how the tools are structured:

✧ **Credit Cards** are a form of *revolving* debt. You borrow, repay, then borrow again. But interest compounds **daily**.

This makes them the most dangerous if not paid in full each month.

Credit card interest **is calculated daily**, not monthly.

Here's how it works in practice:

1. **Daily Balance Method**
    - Your credit card company calculates your balance **each day**.
    - They take your **APR**, divide it by 365 to get the **daily periodic rate**.
      Example: 18.99% ÷ 365 ≈ **0.052% per day**.
2. **Daily Interest Accrual**
    - Each day, they multiply your balance by the daily rate and add that interest to your running total for the month.
    - If you don't pay your balance in full, interest is added **to your balance** — and the next day's interest is calculated on the new, slightly larger balance. That's **daily compounding**.
3. **At the End of the Billing Cycle**
    - All those daily interest charges are summed up and posted to your account as one total **interest charge**.
    - Then, your next month starts with that new, higher balance — unless you've paid enough to cover it.

Why this matters:

If you make a payment **mid-cycle**, your daily balance drops immediately, which reduces the interest you accumulate for the rest of that billing period. This is why **paying more often than once a month** can save you money on interest.

Here's the **daily interest accumulation** for a **$1,000 credit card balance at 18.99% APR** over a 30-day month, with interest added daily

Day	Balance	Interest Added
1	$1,000.52	$0.52
2	$1,001.04	$0.52
3	$1,001.56	$0.52
...	...	...
28	$1,014.67	$0.53
29	$1,015.20	$0.53
30	$1,015.73	$0.53
Payment	**$990.73**	—

Summary for the Month

- **Starting Balance:** $1,000.00
- **Ending Balance Before Payment:** $1,015.73
- **Total Interest Added This Month:** $15.73
- **Minimum Payment (2% or $25 min):** $25.00
- **Principal Paid:** $9.27
- **Ending Balance After Payment:** $990.73

What this shows:

Even though you made the minimum payment of $25, **over 60%** of it went to interest for the month, and only **$9.27** reduced the actual debt. The next month, interest will again accumulate **daily** on $990.73, keeping you in debt for years if you stick to minimums. This book is written to show you how to AVOID this scenario !

✧**Personal Loans / Auto Loans** are *installment* loans. You borrow a lump sum and repay over time. Interest is often fixed and follows an amortization schedule.

How It Works

1. **Lump Sum Borrowing**
   With a personal loan or auto loan, the lender gives you the full loan amount (the **principal**) upfront.
   - Personal loans can be used for almost anything (debt consolidation, home repairs, medical bills).
   - Auto loans are tied to a specific vehicle purchase.
2. **Fixed Interest**
   Most of these loans have a **fixed interest rate** — the percentage you pay the lender for borrowing the money.
   - Because the rate is fixed, your monthly payment stays the same throughout the life of the loan.

- This makes it predictable and easier to budget for.

3. **Amortization Schedule (See above)**
   An amortization schedule is like a payment blueprint for the loan:

   - It shows how each monthly payment is split between **interest** and **principal**.
   - In the **early months**, most of your payment goes toward interest, and only a small part reduces the principal.
   - In the **later months**, the opposite happens — more of your payment goes to principal because the interest is calculated on a smaller remaining balance.

Example:

If you borrow $10,000 for 5 years at 7% APR:

- First payment: About **$58** goes to interest, **$140** to principal.
- Midway through: About **$33** to interest, **$165** to principal.
- Last payment: Almost all of it goes to principal.

Why It Matters

Predictable Payments

- Fixed interest and an amortization schedule mean you know exactly how much you owe each month — no surprises.
- This helps with budgeting and planning other financial goals.

Total Interest Cost

- Because interest is front-loaded in the early months, paying extra toward the principal early on can **dramatically reduce the total interest paid** and shorten the loan term.
- Example: Paying an extra $100/month on a 5-year loan could shave a year off repayment and save hundreds in interest.

Different from Credit Cards

- Installment loans have a set payoff date — you can see the end of the tunnel.
- Credit cards are **revolving credit** with no fixed payoff date, and interest can vary monthly.

Lines of Credit (LOCs) function like credit cards but often have lower interest rates. They can be powerful tools if used strategically—but dangerous if treated like "free money."

How It Works

A **Line of Credit (LOC)** is a flexible borrowing account.

- The bank sets a **maximum amount** you can borrow (your credit limit).
- You can **borrow, repay, and borrow again** as needed — similar to how a credit card works.
- You only pay interest on the amount you actually use, not the whole limit.

Example:

- Your LOC limit: **$10,000**
- You use $3,000 for home repairs.
- You only pay interest on the $3,000 — not the full $10,000.
- If you pay back $1,000, your available credit goes up to $8,000, and you can borrow again without reapplying.

LOCs can be:

- **Personal LOC** — unsecured, based on your creditworthiness.
- **Home Equity LOC (HELOC)** — secured by your home's value.

- **Business LOC** — for small business expenses.

Real world example of how a LOC works:

A **Line of Credit (LOC)** linked to your checking account works like an invisible safety net. Imagine you have $200 in your checking account, and your LOC has a $5,000 limit. You write a check for $500 to pay your rent. Normally, your account would go negative — but with the LOC, the bank automatically transfers $300 from the credit line into your checking account to cover the shortfall. This keeps your account from bouncing and avoids overdraft fees, but now you owe $300 on the LOC. From that day, interest starts accumulating **only on the $300 you used**, not the full $5,000 limit. If your next paycheck of $1,000 is deposited, the bank can automatically pay back the $300 plus interest, and the LOC balance returns to zero — ready for future use. In practice, your statement will show money flowing **in from the LOC when you overspend** and **out to repay it when you deposit funds**, almost like a revolving door of cash.

Day	Event	Checking Balance Before	LOC Balance Before	Amount	Interest Today	Checking Balance After	LOC Balance After
1	Rent Payment (LOC Advance $300.00)	$200.00	$0.00	-$500.00	$0.00	$0.00	$300.00

5	Grocery Shopping (LOC Advance $120.00)	$0.00	$300.30	-$120.00	$0.07	$0.00	$420.30
10	Paycheck Deposit	$0.00	$420.81	$1,000.00	$0.10	$579.19	$0.00
15	Car Repair (LOC Advance $20.81)	$579.19	$0.00	-$600.00	$0.00	$0.00	$20.81
20	Online Shopping (LOC Advance $250.00)	$0.00	$20.84	-$250.00	$0.01	$0.00	$270.84

Why It Matters

Potential Benefits

- **Lower interest rates** than most credit cards — makes them useful for covering large short-term costs.
- **Flexibility** — borrow only what you need, when you need it.
- **No fixed payments** like an installment loan — you can pay it off early without penalty.

Potential Dangers

- If you treat it like "free money" and keep borrowing without a plan, you can **end up in a debt cycle**.
- The flexibility can be tempting — small purchases here and there can quietly add up to a big balance.
- If it's secured (like a HELOC), missing payments could put your **home or assets at risk**.

> *A LOC can be a smart financial tool for emergencies or planned expenses* **if you use it with discipline**. *Without discipline, it's just as dangerous as running up a credit card — but the stakes can be even higher.*

Which one traps you faster? Credit cards. Because they make it easy to spend small, feel in control, and stay unaware of how fast the interest builds.

> **"Debt traps you most when it looks harmless"**

3.4– Your Money, Your Power: Don't Let It Sit and Shrink

Unless you're working with a specific **credit-building strategy** (like the customized ones offered at Shopunlocked), holding large amounts of cash as a guarantee or in low-yield accounts often hurts more than it helps.

Why? Because of **inflation**.

If inflation is 5%, and your savings account or CD earns 1%, your money is actually **losing 4% in value every year**.

Now, let's say you have $5,000 sitting in a CD earning 2%, while you owe $5,000 on a credit card at 24.99% interest.

- You're **earning** $100 in a year ($5,000 × 2%)
- But you're **paying** $1,250 in a year ($5,000 × 25%)

That's a net loss of **$1,150**—just for keeping your money "safe."

> *Debt repayment is often the highest guaranteed return on your money.*

Unless your guaranteed CD account pays more than inflation **and/plus** more than the cost of your debt (it rarely does), your best move is to use that money to lower or eliminate your debt balances.

🔧 Real-Life Example:

"I have $3,000 saved as a 'security deposit' for a future apartment. But I'm paying 22% on my $2,500 credit card. That card is costing me over $550/year in interest. If I pay it off now and slowly rebuild my deposit in 6–8 months, I'll have saved more in interest than I'd earn by keeping that money sitting idle."

Result: You reclaim your monthly cash flow, reduce anxiety, and avoid throwing away money on compounding interest.

Of course, make sure you keep a small emergency buffer—but don't overvalue cash that's earning less than your debt is costing.

3.5– The illusion of "manageable" debt

▧ Self-Check: Check Your "Invisible" Interest

Purpose: Realize how much money is silently leaving through interest.

Steps:

1. Choose one credit card or loan.
2. Look at last month's statement.
3. Note the interest paid that month.
4. Multiply by 12 = Annual silent loss.

Below is an example of where you can find the real interest rate you are paying on your card. See your last 3 statements.

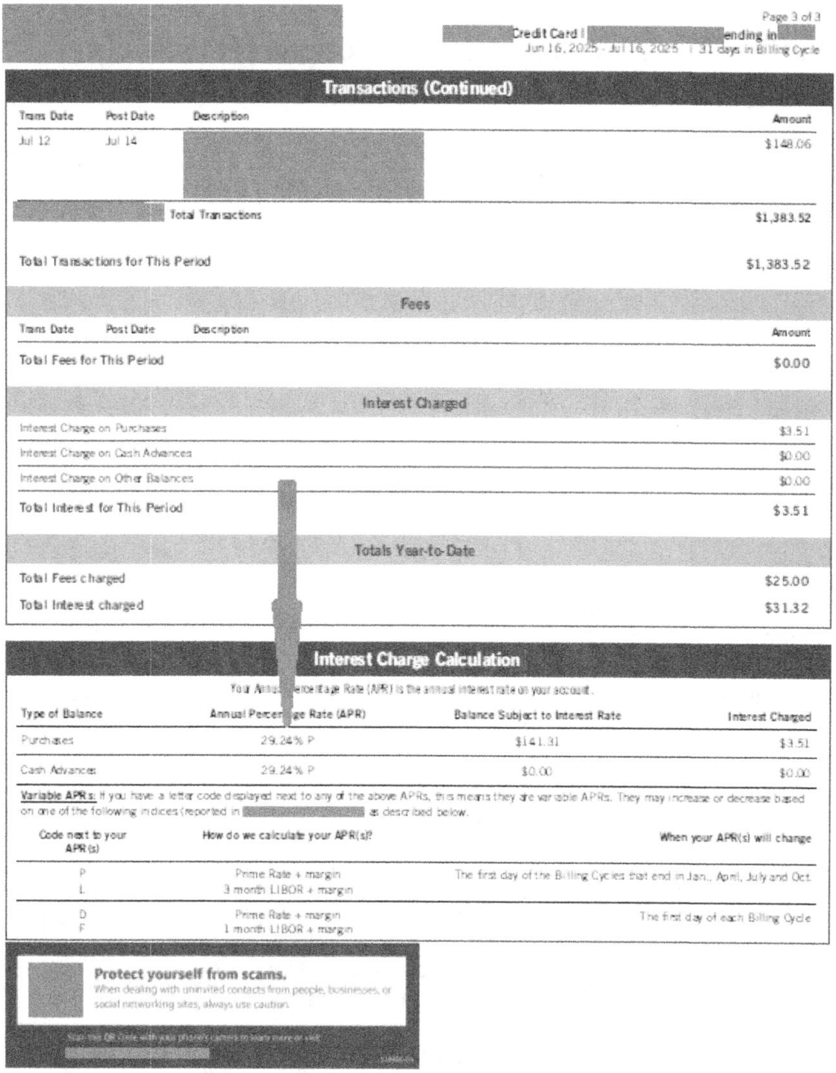

[redacted]

Page 3 of 3

[redacted] Credit Card [redacted] ending in [redacted]
Jun 16, 2025 - Jul 16, 2025 | 31 days in Billing Cycle

Transactions (Continued)

Trans Date	Post Date	Description	Amount
Jul 12	Jul 14	[redacted]	$148.06
[redacted]		Total Transactions	$1,383.52
Total Transactions for This Period			$1,383.52

Fees

Trans Date	Post Date	Description	Amount
Total Fees for This Period			$0.00

Interest Charged

Interest Charge on Purchases	$3.51
Interest Charge on Cash Advances	$0.00
Interest Charge on Other Balances	$0.00
Total Interest for This Period	$3.51

Totals Year-to-Date

Total Fees charged	$25.00
Total Interest charged	$31.32

Interest Charge Calculation

Your Annu[illegible]ercentage Rate (APR) is the annual interest rate on your account.

Type of Balance	Annual Percen[illegible]ge Rate (APR)	Balance Subject to Interest Rate	Interest Charged
Purchases	29.24% P	$141.31	$3.51
Cash Advances	29.24% P	$0.00	$0.00

Variable APRs: If you have a letter code displayed next to any of the above APRs, this means they are variable APRs. They may increase or decrease based on one of the following indices (reported in [redacted] as described below.

Code next to your APR(s)	How do we calculate your APR(s)?	When your APR(s) will change
P L	Prime Rate + margin 3 month LIBOR + margin	The first day of the Billing Cycles that end in Jan., April, July and Oct.
D F	Prime Rate + margin 1 month LIBOR + margin	The first day of each Billing Cycle

Protect yourself from scams.
When dealing with uninvited contacts from people, businesses, or social networking sites, always use caution.

[redacted]

Short Exercise: Take a note of how much interest you paid last month, for each of your cards

🗒 Example:

- Last month: $97 in interest

- Yearly cost: $97 x 12 = **$1,164/year**

That's over a thousand dollars—not going to savings, groceries, or fun... just to the lender.

> *"Debt weighs more than dollars. But healing it sets you free in every direction."*

3.6 Compare and Choose wisely

Topic	Definition	Key Features	Why It Matters	Example
Secured vs. Unsecured Debt	Secured: Backed by collateral (e.g., a car, house). Unsecured: No collateral; lender relies on creditworthiness.	Secured = lower interest, repossession risk. Unsecured = higher rates, harder to collect.	Collateral reduces lender's risk, affects interest rate & approval odds.	Secured: Auto loan. Unsecured: Credit card.
Revolving vs. Installment Debt	Revolving: Borrow, repay, borrow again within a limit. Installment: Fixed loan amount repaid over time.	Revolving = flexible payments, variable interest. Installment = fixed payment schedule.	Impacts credit score differently; revolving debt utilization is a major score factor.	Revolving: Credit card. Installment: Mortgage.
Credit Card Interest	Interest charged on unpaid balance, calculated daily, billed monthly.	High APR (15%–30%), compounding interest, minimum payments extend payoff time.	Daily compounding means debt grows quickly; paying more than the minimum is critical.	$5,000 at 24% APR can take 20+ years to pay with minimums.

Student Loans	Debt for education costs, federal or private.	May have grace periods, income-based repayment, possible deferment/forbearance.	Affects long-term finances; usually not dischargeable in bankruptcy.	Federal Direct Loan with income-driven repayment.
DTI (Debt-to-Income) as Qualifying Metric	Percentage of gross monthly income used for debt payments.	Lenders use thresholds (e.g., <36% for mortgages) to assess ability to repay.	High DTI can block loan approvals or result in worse terms.	$1,800 total debt / $5,000 income = 36% DTI.
Mortgage vs. Personal Loan	Mortgage = secured by property, long term (15–30 years). Personal loan = unsecured, short term (2–7 years).	Mortgage = lower rates, strict approval. Personal = higher rates, faster funding.	Choosing wrong loan type can cost thousands in interest.	Mortgage for home purchase vs. personal loan for renovations.
How Debt Is Applied (Front-Loaded or Not)	Method of applying interest & principal over loan life.	Installment loans often front-load interest (more interest early). Revolving debt interest recalculated monthly.	Front-loading means early payments reduce principal slowly; affects payoff strategies.	Auto loan amortization vs. credit card interest cycle.

Now that you understand the mechanics of debt, let's pull back the curtain in the coming chapters to see how banks use these mechanics to their advantage.

Topics Covered:

- Secured vs. unsecured debt
- Revolving vs. installment debt
- Credit card interest
- Student loans

- DTI as a qualifying metric
- Mortgage vs. personal loan difference
- How debt is applied (front loaded or not)

Key Takeaways

- **Debt creates emotional burnout.** It keeps your body in survival mode and robs you of rest.
- **Debt builds walls between people.** It affects how you love, argue, and show up.
- **Debt delays your dreams.** You deserve a life where your choices aren't chained to balances.
- **Your inner voice matters.** Change how you talk to yourself, and you'll change how you treat your money.
- **Emotional spending comes from unmet needs.** Recognizing those needs gives you back your power.

Specially for you

> *"You don't owe interest for being human. You owe it because no one taught you the system. Now you know. And now you change."*

🔗 Ready to Test Your Knowledge?

☑️ QUIZ 2: Navigating the Debt Landscape

Purpose:

Assess your understanding of different types of debt (secured vs. unsecured), how interest is applied, debt classifications (installment vs. revolving), and strategic concepts like debt-to-income thresholds.

📌 Chapter Summary: What You've Conquered

The system profits from your confusion. But now you have clarity—and clarity is power."

- **Why minimum payments don't reduce your balance.** Most of what you're paying is interest—not progress.
- **How amortization hides your true cost.** Equal payments don't mean equal payoff.
- **The difference between credit cards, loans, and lines of credit.** Each has a different structure—and a different risk.

- **Why slow payoff makes banks rich.** You're being sold convenience at the cost of your future.
- **How to calculate your interest loss.** Awareness is your first financial win.

✹ Next Step

In Chapter 4, we'll finally talk about the **emotional toll of debt**, how it impacts relationships, mental health, and self-worth—and how to begin healing that burden from the inside out.

CHAPTER 4

Debt's Impact on Your Life

When Debt Affects More Than Your Wallet

☑ 4.1– Emotional Burnout: The Silent Weight You Carry

✦ Monica kept telling herself it was fine. The credit card was under control. She hadn't defaulted. She paid something every month. But she couldn't remember the last time she fell asleep without her brain racing about money. She couldn't remember the last time she didn't feel guilt ordering lunch or skipping a bill.

Debt doesn't just live in your wallet. It lives in your chest, your jaw, your back. It shows up as tension headaches, insomnia, or snapping at loved ones.

When every choice you make is filtered through the question *"Can I afford this?"*—you stop feeling free. You stop feeling safe. And over time, you stop dreaming.

> *Debt can keep you financially stable on the outside, while emotionally drowning you on the inside.*

🔄 Rewire Your Story

If you've told yourself, *"It's just stress, I'll deal with it later,"* it might be your brain trying to protect you from being overwhelmed. But emotional avoidance adds pressure. Your body carries what your voice avoids.

Say this instead:

> *"This stress is real. But I'm not powerless.*
> *Every step I take is restoring my peace."*

🔍 4.2– Relationship Friction: When Money Builds Walls

- Hiding purchases
- Arguments about money
- Feelings of guilt or resentment
- Anxiety, avoidance, and the mental burden of debt
- Emotional spending triggers

Money doesn't just affect your personal health—it impacts the way you show up in your relationships.

When you're in debt:

- You might hide purchases to avoid arguments.
- You might start fights over small expenses because you're triggered by scarcity.
- You might feel too ashamed to talk about finances at all.

Money becomes the secret you keep or the weapon you use. Over time, guilt turns into distance, and fear turns into silence.

Debt affects trust, intimacy, and communication—even if it's never directly talked about.

Let's not forget emotional triggers:

- Feeling like a burden in your own household.
- Buying things to make up for saying no.
- Avoiding checking your bank app because it means facing a fight or a fear.

> *Money arguments are rarely about money. They're about fear, power, and protection.*

▧ Self-Check: Emotional Budget Check

Purpose: Identify emotional spending habits that could be hurting you.

Steps:

1. List 5 purchases from last month that weren't needs.
2. What emotion triggered each one? (Stress, joy, boredom, peer pressure?)
3. Was there guilt after? Did it help long-term?

Example:

- New shoes: $89 → Emotion: "I wanted to feel good for a date." → Guilt: "Yes" → Long-term effect: "Still in debt."

Fill out this table with your own information:

Item Purchased	Emotion ?	Guilt ?	Long-Term Effect ?

🔄 Rewire Your Story

If you've been avoiding financial conversations because they cause fights, remind yourself:

> *"I don't have to suffer in silence. I can invite truth without shame."*

💔 4.3– Missed Opportunities: What Debt Silently Steals

At first, it's subtle. You tell yourself, "I'll take that course later."
You think, "Maybe I'll leave this job once things calm down."
You whisper, "Next year I'll start that business."

But weeks turn into months. Months turn into years. And under the surface, your potential—the ideas, the dreams, the changes you once believed were possible—begin to dry up.

Debt is not just about owing money.
It's about **delaying access to your own life.**

🎯 When Debt Becomes the Default Decision-Maker

People don't stay in toxic jobs because they love them.

They stay because of rent, car notes, and credit card minimums.

People don't stop building dreams because they lack ambition.

They stop because **debt keeps interrupting the plan.**

You can't save for the house when every extra dollar is covering last month's interest.

You can't invest for the future when the present is full of payment due dates.

It's not about not having vision—it's about not having margin.

Do you feel you:

- Can't invest
- Can't save for goals
- Can't leave toxic jobs or environments

Have you ever wanted to:

- Start a small business?
- Take a break from a toxic job?
- Go back to school?
- Move out of a stressful living situation?
- Travel or invest?

Debt often puts all of that on pause. When you're living to pay others, you delay your own goals. Your time, energy, and money are spoken for before you get to choose.

> *Debt is not just a bill. It's a delay. A cage. A quiet thief of possibilities.*

And that's why this chapter matters.

Because when you realize how debt is shaping your everyday *and* your future—you start fighting for both.

💭 The Emotional Consequences of Missed Opportunities

After a while, the internal dialogue shifts:

"Maybe I'm just not meant for more."

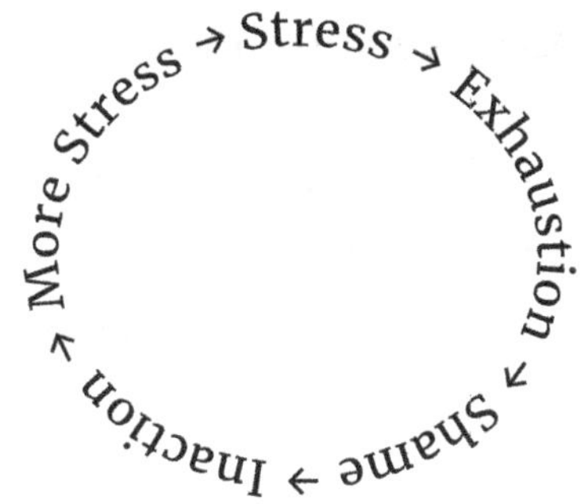

"Other people can afford to dream—I can't."

"Maybe I missed my window."

These thoughts aren't true—but they **feel** true. Because the weight of revolving debt trains your brain to live small, play safe, and avoid risk.

You begin to operate from survival mode, not creativity.
You silence your imagination.
You stop stretching.

🧠 Rewire Your Story

If you've felt stuck in place, it's not because you're lazy or unmotivated. It's because **debt creates a trauma loop**:

To break that loop, we have to give the brain a new truth to anchor:

> ✦ *"I am not broken—I've been financially bound. But the door is still open."*
>
> ✦ *"Every dollar I free from debt is a brick I'm laying toward my freedom."*
>
> ✦ *"I don't have to wait for a better time. This is the better time."*

Visualize one opportunity you thought was no longer available.
Now picture yourself having the income margin and emotional space to say yes to it.
Write it down. Pin it where you can see it.

____
____
____
____
____
____
____
____
____
____
____
____
____
____

That's what we're working towards. Not just $0 balance—**full-option living.**

> *Debt doesn't just delay dreams—it reshapes your life without your permission.*

It changes how you choose jobs. Instead of pursuing a passion or leaving a toxic environment, you might stay because you "can't afford to risk it."

It changes how you parent. You might feel pressured to provide everything, but the stress of keeping up financially prevents you from being emotionally present.

It changes how you dream. The big idea you once had—a side business, a return to school, a solo trip—gets pushed back "until things are better." But for many, "better" never comes... because debt silently absorbs every extra dollar and ounce of mental space.

Missed opportunities don't just cost money—they cost confidence. Over time, you start to believe:

"Maybe I'm not meant for that life."

But here's the truth: You were never unqualified. You were just **occupied.** Occupied by survival-mode. Occupied by interest payments. Occupied by shame.

> *Debt doesn't just steal money—it steals your momentum, your magic, and your options.*

This isn't just about wiping balances. This is about unlocking your life.

🔄 Rewire Your Story

Say this to yourself:

> *"My life deserves options. My dreams matter. Paying off this debt is not just about numbers—it's about reclaiming choice."*

Say this to yourself:

> *"My ideas matter. My future matters. I have permission to want more. Paying off debt is not a punishment—it's my pathway to full possibility."*

Debt limits what you can do, how you feel, and even how you see yourself. But once you break free, the story flips. In Chapter 6, we'll see what life looks like when your income is truly yours again

📌 Chapter Summary: What You've Conquered

> *Debt weighs more than dollars. But healing it sets you free in every direction.*

- **Debt creates emotional burnout.** It keeps your body in survival mode and robs you of rest.
- **Debt builds walls between people.** It affects how you love, argue, and show up.
- **Debt delays your dreams.** You deserve a life where your choices aren't chained to balances.
- **Your inner voice matters.** Change how you talk to yourself, and you'll change how you treat your money.

- **Emotional spending comes from unmet needs.** Recognizing those needs gives you back your power.

💥 Next Step

In Chapter 5, we'll break down exactly **who profits from your debt**—and why they work so hard to keep you confused, comfortable, and paying forever. Knowledge is power. And we're about to reclaim it.

This page is left intentionally blank

CHAPTER 5

Who's Really Profiting?

Who Wins When You Lose?

5.1– Financial Institutions Know Exactly What They're Doing

- How they design statements
- Why rewards programs keep you spending
- The lie of the CD savings vs. credit card debt

How we cooperate with our own financial imprisonment without realizing it.

> *"I thought I was doing great because I hadn't missed a payment in years... but somehow my balance never seemed to shrink."*

That's what Andrea, a 36-year-old social worker, told me during a coaching session. She used her credit card for everyday expenses—groceries, gas, the occasional lunch out. She made her minimum payments every single month. Never late. Never skipped.

And yet, after five years, her $6,000 balance had barely moved.

Why? Because the system wasn't built to help her get out—it was built to keep her paying.

🔍 The Hidden Psychology of Credit Card Design

Credit card companies are **not in the business of helping you build credit**. They're in the business of getting you to:

- **Spend more than you have**
- **Pay interest longer than you should**
- **Feel good while doing it**

Let's break it down:

📃 The Statement Trap:

Ever wonder why your credit card bill says "Minimum Due: $47.29" in big bold letters—but the actual balance is hidden at the bottom?

That's no accident. The layout is designed to psychologically nudge you into **paying less**, so the debt sticks around longer. Less friction for you. More profit for them.

🎁 The Rewards Illusion:

"Get 3% cash back on groceries!"
"Earn miles for every dollar spent!"

Sounds great—until you realize you're spending **18% to 29.99% in interest** just to get **1.5% back**.

It's like buying a $5 coffee with a 30% tip... every time... forever.

🏦 The "Safe" CD Myth:

Many people, like Sonia in the real-life example later in this chapter, are told to never touch their savings—even when their savings earn 4% interest, while they pay 22.99% on credit card debt.

That's **not saving**—that's silently bleeding money.

🔄 Rewire Your Story

If you've ever thought:

"At least I'm not behind."
"At least I'm earning points."

Try saying:

> *"This game wasn't designed for me to win. But I'm learning the rules now—and I choose a new way."*

🧠 Real-Life Case: Sonia's CD vs. Credit Card Trap

Interest traps and how banks profit.

✦Meet Sonia✦

She's 42, works in healthcare, and has always been told by her parents: *'Never touch your savings no matter what.'*

Sonia is proud of her $10,000 Certificate of Deposit (CD), locked up for 12 months earning a 4% interest rate.

But here's the kicker:

She also owes $8,000 on a credit card that charges her 22.99% interest. She pays only the minimum: about $200/month. In total, she'll end up paying over $6,000 in interest if she sticks to that plan.

Meanwhile, her CD will earn her around $400 that year. So, she's earning $400 while giving away $6,000. Who's winning?

👉 **Bottom line**: Sonia is keeping money "safe" while her debt is burning a hole through her financial life.

> 💡 *"That CD is not helping. It's hurting. Use it to pay off high-interest debt. Then rebuild later—faster and freer."*

▧ Self-Check: CD vs. Credit Card Showdown

Purpose: Help you rethink the true value of "saving" when you're also carrying high-interest debt.

Steps:

1. Note your CD or savings value and APY (% interest earned).
2. Note your highest debt balance and APR (% interest charged).
3. Calculate interest earned vs. interest paid annually.
4. Compare: Which is costing/gaining more?

Example:

- CD: $10,000 @ 4% = $400/year
- Credit card: $8,000 @ 22.99% = $1,839.20/year
- **You're losing $1,439.20 annually.**

Item	Balance	Interest Rate	Annual Interest (Cost or Gain)
CD (Savings)	$10,000	4%	**+$400** (earnings)
Credit Card	$8,000	22.99%	**–$1,839.20** (cost)

Net Effect (Gain vs. Loss)

- **Total Gain from CD**: +$400
- **Total Cost from Credit Card**: –$1,839.20
- **Net Result**: **–$1,439.20** (overall loss)

👉 In plain words: even though your CD earns you $400 a year, your credit card costs you **over 4.5 times more** in interest. You're left with a net **loss of $1,439.20** annually.

5.2– The Business of Debt

- Lending is one of the most profitable industries
- Lenders get rich from your minimum payments - How banks make billions on your delay

Why Paying Slowly Is Profitable (for Them)

Let's be blunt: **debt is a product**. It's packaged, priced, and sold—**and you are the revenue stream.**

Every time you:

- Make the minimum payment
- Carry a balance
- Delay payoff

You're making someone else richer. Usually a bank, hedge fund, or lender's bonus pool.

They depend on **your slow progress**.

💸 Why Minimum Payments Are the Sweet Spot—for Them

Say you owe $5,000 on a card at 19.99% APR. If you only make minimum payments, it could take you **20+ years** to pay it off—and you'll pay nearly **$7,000 in interest.**

That $5,000 turns into **$12,000.**
Not because you bought more—but because they designed it that way.

> 💡 *"Lenders don't need you to default. They just need you to drag your feet."*
>
> 💡 **0% Interest Offers**: *The Danger Behind the Deal*

Let's talk about those tempting **0% interest promotions**—credit card balance transfers, store financing, "no interest for 12 months" offers. They sound like a golden opportunity. And sometimes they can be. But only **if you fully understand the fine print** and approach it with a clear strategy.

Here's what most people don't realize:

- Once the promotional period ends, the interest rate usually jumps to the highest rate on the market (often 25–29.99%).
- Many cards charge a **balance transfer fee upfront** (usually 3%–5%).
- If you miss **even one payment**, the promo rate can be **revoked immediately**.
- Only certain transactions (like direct balance transfers) qualify. Purchases or cash advances often rack up interest right away.

🔧 Real-Life Example: Strategy vs. Slippery Slope

Imagine you transfer $4,000 to a new credit card offering 0% interest for 12 months, with a 3% transfer fee.

- Total debt becomes: $4,000 + $120 = **$4,120** [$120 being the 3% transfer fee charged immediately on the day of the debt transfer]
- Now divide by 12 months: $4,120 ÷ 12 = **$343.33/ month**

If you set **$343.33 on autopay**, you'll clear it all before interest kicks in. But if you only pay the minimum ($50–$75), you'll have a large balance remaining—and it could be hit with 29.99% retroactive interest on the **entire amount**.

Here's how a $4,120 balance on a 0% interest card for 15 months would behave if you only made the minimum

payment of $75, and then the APR jumps to 28.99% afterward:

Month	Starting Balance	Interest Rate	Interest This Month	Payment	Ending Balance
1	$4,120.00	0.00%	$0.00	$75.00	$4,045.00
2	$4,045.00	0.00%	$0.00	$75.00	$3,970.00
3	$3,970.00	0.00%	$0.00	$75.00	$3,895.00
4	$3,895.00	0.00%	$0.00	$75.00	$3,820.00
5	$3,820.00	0.00%	$0.00	$75.00	$3,745.00
6	$3,745.00	0.00%	$0.00	$75.00	$3,670.00
7	$3,670.00	0.00%	$0.00	$75.00	$3,595.00
8	$3,595.00	0.00%	$0.00	$75.00	$3,520.00
9	$3,520.00	0.00%	$0.00	$75.00	$3,445.00
10	$3,445.00	0.00%	$0.00	$75.00	$3,370.00
11	$3,370.00	0.00%	$0.00	$75.00	$3,295.00
12	$3,295.00	0.00%	$0.00	$75.00	$3,220.00
13	$3,220.00	0.00%	$0.00	$75.00	$3,145.00
14	$3,145.00	0.00%	$0.00	$75.00	$3,070.00
15	$3,070.00	0.00%	$0.00	$75.00	$2,995.00
16	$2,995.00	28.99%	$72.31	$75.00	$2,992.31
17	$2,992.31	28.99%	$72.23	$75.00	$2,989.54
18	$2,989.54	28.99%	$72.16	$75.00	$2,986.70
19	$2,986.70	28.99%	$72.08	$75.00	$2,983.78
20	$2,983.78	28.99%	$72.01	$75.00	$2,980.79

Why this matters:

- During the 0% promo period, your balance only falls by the payment amount.
- Once 28.99% interest kicks in, most of your $75 payment goes to interest.

- As you can see by month 20, the balance is barely moving — you're stuck in a debt trap where payments mostly feed the lender.

Pro Tip: When you have a 0% interest credit card for a promotional period of 15 to 18 months, if you can split the balance over 8 or 12 months instead of 15 to 18, even better. The faster you eliminate the balance, the less risk.

Once the debt is gone, don't use that card again. It's now a **high-interest product**. But don't close the account either—it helps your credit score to keep it open with zero balance.

Want more advanced strategies like this? Check out **Shopunlocked's book on credit management**.

Banks profit most from your **slowest efforts**. That's why:

- They encourage minimum payments
- Offer "easy monthly terms"
- Make it hard to understand how interest accumulates

Debt companies don't want you to default. They want you to just stay "afloat" enough to keep paying interest for years.

This is why minimum payments are dangerous. They seem helpful—*"Just $75 a month!"*—but that $75 might only reduce your debt by $5.

The illusion of manageable debt is what keeps people stuck.

🔄 Rewire Your Story

If you've been proud of just staying "caught up," that's valid. You've been doing your best. But now, you upgrade that narrative:

> *"I'm not here to survive debt.*
> *I'm here to eliminate it."*

▧ Self-Check: Who's Winning—You or the Bank?

Purpose: To see the real scoreboard, not just the rewards.

Steps:

1. Look at your last 12 months statement. Calculate how much interest you've paid over these last 12 months
2. List all cash-back, points, or rewards you received.
3. Compare cost vs. reward. Who's really winning?

Example:

- Interest paid: $800
- Rewards earned: $56
- Net result: –$744 loss

🔄 Rewire Your Story

If you've ever said:

"I like the perks, though."

Say this instead:

> *"The perks are crumbs. I'm done mistaking crumbs for a feast."*

5.3– Common Tricks Used Against You

- Teaser rates
- Balance transfer catches
- Late fees, over-limit fees

Teaser Rates: "0% for 6 months!" But if you miss a payment—or carry a balance after month 6? You're retroactively charged 24.99% on the **entire** balance.

Balance Transfers: 0% sounds good, but the 3%–5% **transfer fee** adds up—and many people don't pay it off in time, triggering high penalty rates.

Late Fees & Overlimit Charges: You're charged $35 for being 3 days late... and your APR jumps. It's not about teaching you a lesson. It's about maximizing revenue.

5.4– Understanding the Terms They Don't Explain

Let's simplify the jargon:

- **Revolving Credit:** Debt you can carry over month to month (like credit cards). Flexible but dangerous.

- **Installment Loan:** Fixed-term loans (like mortgages or car loans) with set payments.
- **APY (Annual Percentage Yield):** What you earn on savings.
- **APR (Annual Percentage Rate):** What you pay on debt.
- **Intro APR:** A temporary low interest rate—**not forever. Always expires.**

📌 Chapter Summary: What You've Conquered

> *Debt isn't just a math problem. It's a money-making machine—and you've been its fuel. But now you see it. And now you stop feeding it.*

- **Credit card companies don't want you to fail—just to slow-walk your progress.** The longer you linger in minimum payments, the longer they profit.
- **Reward programs are not your friends.** A few points or miles can never make up for thousands of dollars in interest.
- **You might be saving... while still losing.** Keeping money locked in a 4% CD while paying 22% interest on debt is a silent, costly mistake.
- **Lenders depend on delay.** Their entire business is built on your hesitation, your emotional overwhelm, and your lack of time to do the math.

- **They use every trick available—because they work.** Teaser rates that vanish, balance transfers with fine print, fees for being a few dollars over or a few days late... It's not about discipline. It's about design.
- **Even your statement layout is engineered.** Bolded minimums, hidden totals—everything is meant to make spending feel good and paying feel optional.
- **The words matter.** Understanding terms like APR, APY, revolving credit, and installment debt gives you the power to stop playing blindly.

> 💡 *The game only works when you don't know you're playing. But now you do. And that changes everything.*

✸ Next Step

In Chapter 6, we'll shift the focus back to **you.**
What does life look like after debt? What can you actually do with your income when it's yours again?

Let's talk about freedom—not just from debt, but toward **real financial peace.**

This page is left intentionally blank

CHAPTER 6

Debt-Free Living = Choice = Freedom

6.1– What Changes When You don't have debt to pay back anymore.

> *"For the first time in years, I wasn't planning my whole month around what I owed. I was planning around what I wanted."*

That's how James described the moment he made his final credit card payment. It wasn't dramatic. No fireworks. No parade. Just a quiet click of "Submit Payment." And a feeling he hadn't felt in over a decade:

Freedom.

Because that's what debt takes first—**your ability to choose.** It decides how much of your paycheck you keep, how many risks you can take, how long you stay in jobs or relationships that no longer fit.

🔍 Life Without Debt: What Changes Instantly

When you're no longer living under a pile of payments, three things shift—fast:

1. **More Options, Less Fear**
   You can leave a toxic job. Take a week off without guilt. Invest in something that lights you up—because your money isn't already spoken for.

2. **Your Income Feels Like Yours Again**
   A paycheck without deductions for loans or credit cards feels different. You realize how much you were giving away—and how fast you can build when you stop.

3. **Peace of Mind = Energy for Life**
   No more late-night mental math. No more dodging the mailbox or bank notifications. Your brain gets quieter. Your body gets lighter. Your energy goes toward creating, not coping.

⚖️ The Strange Side of Freedom

Here's the truth most people won't admit: being debt free can actually feel *weird*. If you've lived for years under stress, juggling bills and putting out fires, the calm can feel "boring." Your brain is wired to expect chaos, so when the noise is gone, some people unconsciously recreate it—by swiping the card again, taking on loans, or jumping into unnecessary expenses. They "feel too free, too good," and slip back into debt just to feel the rush of movement. That's why debt freedom isn't just about paying balances—it's about learning to live in peace, to get comfortable with stability, and to recognize that quiet is not emptiness, it's opportunity.

✏ Self-Check: Are You Addicted to Financial Chaos?

Take a pause and ask yourself:

1. Do I feel restless when things are calm with my money?
2. Do I catch myself looking for "just one more purchase" even when I don't need it?
3. Do I miss the urgency of juggling payments, as if it gave me purpose?
4. When I think of a future without debt, do I imagine boredom instead of freedom?
5. Am I tempted to reward myself with spending the moment I get ahead?

☞ If you answered "yes" to two or more, your challenge isn't just numbers—it's *retraining your brain* to enjoy peace. Real freedom means learning to love stability and replacing the old rush of chaos with the calm power of growth.

🔄 Rewire Your Story

If you've thought:

"Even if I pay this off, nothing will really change..."
"I'll always feel behind..."

Try telling yourself instead:

> *"Debt was a storm. I'm choosing peace. I get to use my money to build joy, not just survive stress."*

Debt-free living isn't just about zero balances. It's about **full control**.

6.2– Real Example: The Family That Became Mortgage-Free Early

✦Tasha and Emmanuel bought their first home in 2010. Their mortgage was $190,000 with a 30-year term. But after five years of minimum payments, they realized most of their money was going toward interest—not equity.

So, they got intentional. With the help of a coach at Shopunlocked:

- They refinanced to a 15-year mortgage.
- Cut unnecessary subscriptions.
- Turned a spare bedroom into a short-term rental.
- Used every tax refund, bonus, and birthday check to make extra payments.

They paid off the entire mortgage in 12 years.

"We saved more than $65,000 in interest," Emmanuel said.

"But the best part? We raised our kids in a house we *owned*. That security... no payment can buy that feeling."

Debt-free living gave their family a **legacy**, not just relief.

6.3– The Snowball Effect of Freedom

Here's the part no one tells you: once you get out of debt, your financial wins get **faster and easier**.

Let's say you used to pay:

- $200 toward a credit card
- $350 toward a car loan
- $800 toward a mortgage

That's $1,350 every month now freed up.

Now, instead of paying lenders, imagine:

- $500/month going into a retirement fund
- $200/month into a child's education account
- $300/month into a business or vacation goal
- $350/month saved for your future peace of mind

Same total ($1,350/month) just allocated towards your future. After one year, that's **$16,200** redirected toward your goals.

> 💡 *"Debt steals your future. Paying it off gets it back—with interest."*

This is the **snowball effect in reverse**: instead of rolling debt downhill, you're rolling momentum upward.

Self-Check: Picture Your Debt-Free Paycheck

Purpose: Connect emotionally and practically with what freedom will feel like.

Steps:

1. List your current monthly debt payments (credit cards, loans, mortgage, etc.).

2. Total the amount.

3. Now imagine that money landing in your account with **no obligations**.
4. Write a paragraph: *"If I had that full amount each month, I would..."*

Example:

- Debt Payments: $1,270/month
- "If I had that money each month, I would finally max out my Roth IRA, take my mom on a trip, and build up my emergency savings to $10,000."

🔄 Rewire Your Story

If you've ever thought:

"People like me don't get ahead. I'll always be playing catch-up."

Say this instead:

> *"Freedom isn't reserved for the lucky. It's earned by choices. And I'm choosing well now."*

💬 Written just for you

> *"Debt is the quiet thief of dreams. But every payment you make is a brick you lay on the road back to freedom."*

📌 Chapter Summary: What You've Conquered

> *Getting out of debt isn't just about numbers. It's about getting your life back—and finally becoming the one who decides what happens next.*

- **Debt-free living unlocks your choices.** When you're no longer paying lenders every month, you stop living in reaction mode and start designing a life that fits your goals, values, and priorities.
- **More options mean less fear.** You can walk away from a toxic job, say yes to new opportunities, or breathe between paychecks without panic. Options give you power—and peace.
- **Your income becomes fully yours again.** Every dollar you earn can now serve *you*, not your creditors. This shift is both emotional and strategic—it feels like a raise without needing a promotion.
- **Peace of mind is real wealth.** When the mental noise of debt quiets down, your energy returns. You sleep better. You think clearer. You smile more. And that clarity opens doors.
- **Momentum builds once payments stop.** That $200 you used to send to a credit card? Now it becomes $200 toward investing, saving, traveling, or giving. Small wins stack fast when you're moving forward instead of catching up.
- **Debt freedom fuels compound growth.** That same $200/month you save on interest can become over $2,000/year in investments—year after year. It's how freedom multiplies.
- **Real people do this every day.** Whether it's a family paying off a mortgage early or someone taking

back control after years of debt, the blueprint is not fantasy. It's action + time + belief.

> 💡 *"Freedom doesn't come from making more—it comes from needing less to feel safe. And that begins the moment your money becomes yours again."*

✸ Next Step

In Chapter 7, we'll talk about how to stay debt-free once you get there—**budgeting as a pre-requisite, planning correctly, and making sure this freedom lasts for life.**

This page is left intentionally blank

CHAPTER 7

From Budgeting to War Plan

Take Control Before You Attack

☑ 7.1- Revisit the 50/30/20 Rule: Your First Weapon

> *"You don't fight a financial battle blindfolded. You fight with a plan."*

Let's start with your first weapon: the budget. Not the kind that feels like punishment. The kind that gives you power.

You may remember this from "*Start With This*" the first book from this series, written by Regine Godefroy **(QR Code below)**. It's worth revisiting now that you're further along in your journey.

The **50/30/20 Rule** isn't a rigid formula. It's a **strategic guide** to help you regain control, build awareness, and finally use your income on purpose.

🔍 The Breakdown:

- **50% = Needs:** Rent, food, utilities, transportation, minimum debt payments
- **30% = Wants:** Subscriptions, entertainment, dining out, non-essentials
- **20% = Savings & Debt Payoff:** Emergency fund, extra loan payments, investing

This framework gives you **permission and direction** at the same time. You still get to enjoy your life—but you also make room for the future.

> 💡 *"Budgeting isn't about restriction. It's about reassigning your energy."*

🔄 Rewire Your Story

If you've ever thought:

"I don't make enough to budget."
"Budgeting won't change anything—I'm too behind."

Tell yourself:

> *"My income is a tool. I'm not too far behind. I'm just starting to look forward."*

Every plan starts with a blueprint. This is yours.

7.2– Why Budgeting Is Not Optional Anymore

Let's be real: debt payoff without budgeting is just wishful thinking.

If you don't know:

- What's coming in
- What's going out
- Where the leaks are

... then you're not in control. The numbers are.

Budgeting isn't optional because **you can't fix what you don't track.**

It's like trying to diet without reading nutrition labels. You might cut a few calories, but you won't make real progress until you know what's *actually* going in.

🔧 How to Track Expenses Like a Pro:

- **Pick your system:** Notebook, spreadsheet, budgeting app—doesn't matter as long as you use it.

- **Choose a window:** Track weekly or monthly, but track consistently.
- **Don't guess. Look.** Check your bank statements and card activity.

> 💡 *"Awareness is your first defense against financial chaos."*

🟫 Self-Check: Budget Readiness Score

Purpose: Quickly assess if you're budgeting at the level you need to be.

Steps (answer with Yes or No):

1. Do you know your total monthly income?
2. Do you track your monthly expenses?
3. Do you plan before spending—or regret after?
4. Do you use a budgeting tool ("Start With This" book, spreadsheet, app, notebook)?
5. Do you adjust when things change?

Results:

- **0–2 out of 5 "Yes":** Budget Beginner → Time to build awareness
- **3–4 out of 5 "Yes":** Budget Learner → You're close—just tighten the system
- **5 out of 5 "Yes":** Budget Boss → Use it now to fuel debt freedom

> 💡 *"You can't fix what you don't track"*

Later, in Chapter 11, we'll go deeper into weekly and monthly cash flow tracking to customize this plan for you

7.3– Budget > Then Pay

A common mistake in debt payoff is skipping straight to action:

"I'm just going to throw all my extra money at the credit card and hope it works out."

The problem? Without a plan, it rarely works:

- You burn out.
- You forget bills.
- You end up using the credit card again because you didn't map out the month.

This is why budgeting must come *before* aggressive payoff. It's the **blueprint**, not the afterthought.

🔧 Fixed vs. Flexible Expenses

When budgeting, categorize each monthly expense as:

- **Fixed:** Rent, car note, insurance, Wi-Fi
- **Flexible:** Eating out, shopping, Netflix, salon visits

This helps you know **what you can change fast**, and what needs long-term adjustment.

▧ Self-Check: Fixed vs. Flexible Spending Sort

Purpose: Pinpoint where your immediate savings can begin.

Steps:

1. List all monthly recurring expenses.
2. Label each as Fixed (non-negotiable) or Flexible (adjustable).
3. Circle the top 2 flexible expenses to cut this month.

Example:

- Netflix – Flexible
- Car Payment – Fixed
- Takeout – Flexible
- Wi-Fi – Fixed

✂ Cut: Takeout & Netflix = +$150/month toward debt payoff

> 💡 *"Small cuts can lead to big momentum."*

🔄 Rewire Your Story

If you've told yourself:

"I hate budgeting. I'm just not that disciplined."

Here's the shift:

> *"Budgeting is not a personality—it's a skill. And like any skill, I can build it with practice."*

You don't need to be perfect. You just need to be aware.

💬 Written just for you

> *"A budget is a battle plan. It doesn't just show you what you owe—it shows you where you can win."*

📌 Chapter Summary: What You've Conquered

> *You can't build freedom without a blueprint. Budgeting is the first brick.*
>
> *Budgeting isn't boring. It's how you stop fighting blind—and start winning on purpose.*

- **Budgeting comes first, always.** Before you attack debt, you need to know exactly what's coming in, what's going out, and where the gaps are. Without a clear plan, you're just throwing money at a problem and hoping it sticks.
- **Guesswork leads to setbacks.** Many people start aggressively paying off debt only to realize mid-month they didn't leave enough for groceries or bills. This leads them right back into more debt. Budgeting protects you from that cycle.
- **The 50/30/20 Rule gives structure to your spending.** It creates balance between your needs,

wants, and goals so you can make progress without feeling punished.

- **Your expenses fall into two camps: fixed and flexible.** When you can quickly identify which ones are non-negotiable and which can be reduced or cut, you start freeing up cash to attack debt faster.
- **Real budgeting reveals your opportunities.** It's not just about cutting—it's about creating. When you see what you've been spending, you begin to see what you could be saving or redirecting toward freedom.
- **Awareness changes everything.** When you stop saying "I don't know where my money goes" and start tracking it, your power returns—line by line, month by month.

> 💡 *"You don't have to budget forever. But if you want to be free forever, you have to budget now."*

✸ Next Step

In Chapter 8, we'll make sure you speak the language of money with clarity. You'll learn the terms most lenders hope you never understand—so you can make smarter, sharper decisions for the rest of your life.

CHAPTER 8

Common Words, Clear Meaning

Speak the Language of Money

☑ 8.1 Why Language Matters

> *"I thought I understood interest—until I realized I'd paid over $6,000 and barely touched my credit card balance."*

Money isn't just emotional. It's also **linguistic.** And if you don't speak the language, you can't negotiate, plan, or protect yourself effectively.

Financial institutions use language like armor. Terms like APR, DTI, amortization, revolving credit—they can sound intimidating or boring on purpose. Because when you don't understand, you're more likely to say "yes" when you should say "wait," or "sure" when you should say "no."

This chapter is your **translation guide.** By the end of it, you'll not only understand the terms—they'll feel like tools. Weapons in your financial war chest.

🔄 Rewire Your Story

If you've ever thought:

> *"I'm not a numbers person. I don't get finance."*

Here's the shift:

> *"This isn't about being good at math. It's about being good to myself. I can learn this. One word at a time."*

☑ 8.2 The Words You Need to Own

Let's break down the most important financial terms in plain, everyday English.

🔍 Interest

The cost of borrowing money.
If you borrow $1,000 at 10% annual interest, it'll cost you $100 a year.

Think of interest as the "rental fee" for using someone else's money.

🔍 Principal

The original amount you borrowed (or the amount still owed on a loan).
If your loan is $10,000, and you've paid $1,000 so far, your principal is still $9,000.

🔍 APR vs. APY

- **APR (Annual Percentage Rate):** What you pay on debt (interest + some fees).
- **APY (Annual Percentage Yield):** What you earn on savings (interest with compounding included).

APR = What it costs you.
APY = What it earns you.

🔍 Amortized Loan

A loan where your monthly payment stays the same, but the amount going toward **interest vs. principal** changes over time.

Early payments go mostly to interest. As you keep on paying, later payments go more toward principal.

🔍 Line of Credit (LOC)

Used strategically, it can be a powerful debt-payoff tool. Used emotionally, it's a trap.

LOC: Your Flexible Friend or Silent Trap?

A **Line of Credit (LOC)** is a type of flexible loan that lets you borrow money **up to a set limit**, repay it, and borrow again as needed. You're only charged interest on the amount you use—not the full limit.

☑ **Advantages:**

- Only pay interest on what you borrow
- Reusable: once repaid, it becomes available again
- Can be used for emergencies, large expenses, or debt payoff strategies (see later in this book)
- Often has lower interest than credit cards

⚠ **Disadvantages:**

- Easy to overuse or treat like "free money"
- Interest rates are usually **variable**, meaning they can increase
- Some LOCs require monthly interest-only payments, so **principal never goes down unless you actively pay more**

💡 *Pro Tip: A LOC can work in your favor* ***only if*** *you use it with a fixed plan and strict discipline.*

🔍 HELOC: Home Equity Line of Credit

A **HELOC** is a specific kind of line of credit **secured by your home.** It allows you to borrow against the equity (value you own) in your house.

Think of it like a second mortgage you can dip into when needed—often at lower interest rates.

☑ **Advantages:**

- Typically **lower interest** than personal loans or credit cards
- Interest may be **tax-deductible** (check current IRS guidelines)
- Can be great for debt consolidation, home improvements, or emergency funding

⚠ **Disadvantages:**

- **Your home is collateral.** If you default, you could lose your home.
- Interest rates are often **variable**
- Requires closing costs or appraisal in some cases
- Tempting to overuse for non-essentials

1. First-Lien HELOC

- Replaces your primary mortgage
- Combines a HELOC and checking account in one
- Can be powerful for rapid mortgage payoff strategies
- Requires excellent discipline and **deep understanding of cash flow**

2. Second-Lien HELOC

- Sits on top of your existing mortgage (like a second layer)
- Less risky, doesn't affect your main mortgage
- Most common and easier to manage for general borrowers

💡 *Always ask: Is the HELOC giving me leverage—or is it just giving me more monthly payments?*

🔍 Credit Card

A revolving line of credit for everyday spending. You borrow money up to a limit and are charged interest if you don't pay it off in full each month.

Convenient—but expensive if misused.

☑ Credit Card Fine Print Decoded

Credit card statements and offers often bury key terms in the fine print. Here's how to read them:

- **"Minimum payment due"** is the *smallest* amount—but paying only that stretches your debt and maximizes interest.
- **"Intro APR"** is temporary. Find out when it ends and what the regular rate will be.
- **"Penalty APR"** is a higher rate triggered if you pay late—sometimes over 29.99%.

- **"Grace period"** is the window to pay in full before interest starts. Miss it once, and every dollar may start accruing interest instantly.
- **"Cash advance APR"** is often higher than your purchase APR and starts accumulating interest **immediately**—no grace period.

💡 *If you don't know what a line in your contract means—assume it benefits the lender, not you.*

🔍 Credit Card Balance Transfer

Moving debt from one credit card to another, often for a promotional 0% interest rate. Be careful: there's usually a **fee (3–5%)**, and interest may spike if not paid on time.

🔍 0% APR

A temporary promotional rate that gives you time to pay off a balance with no interest.
⚠ *It doesn't last. And interest may apply retroactively if you miss a payment or don't pay it off in time.*

🔍 Income

Money coming **in**: wages, freelance pay, tips, benefits, rental income, etc.

🔍 Expense

Money going **out**: bills, food, rent, gas, subscriptions, debt payments, etc.

🔍 Recurring / Fixed / Variable Expenses

- **Recurring:** Bills that come every month (utilities, rent, loan payments).
- **Fixed:** Stay the same each time (car payment, insurance).
- **Variable:** Change monthly (groceries, gas, entertainment).

Knowing the difference helps you cut smart, not blindly.

🔍 Emergency Fund

A cash reserve (ideally 3–6 months of your total expenses) for true emergencies: job loss, medical crisis, urgent repairs.

This should be your first financial goal—before investing or even aggressive debt payoff.

🔍 Snowball vs. Avalanche Method

Two debt payoff strategies (see later in this book):

- **Snowball:** Pay off the smallest debt first. Builds motivation.

- **Avalanche:** Pay off the highest interest debt first. Saves money long-term.

Pick the one that keeps you going. Psychology does matter.

❄️ 8.3 The Snowball Method: Small Wins That Create Big Momentum

☑️ What Is the Snowball Method?

The **Snowball Method** is a popular and psychologically powerful way to eliminate debt. Instead of focusing on the debt with the highest interest rate (like the **Avalanche Method**), you focus on the **smallest balance first**, regardless of the interest rate.

Why? Because **quick wins build confidence**—and confidence fuels momentum.

Imagine rolling a small snowball downhill. At first, it's tiny. But with every rotation, it gathers more snow. Soon it's rolling faster, gaining size, and becoming unstoppable.

That's exactly what this method does with your motivation and your money.

🔧 How the Snowball Method Works (Step-by-Step)

1. **List all your debts** from smallest to largest **by balance**, not interest rate.
2. **Make minimum payments** on all debts—except the smallest.

3. Throw **everything extra** (side hustle money, budget cuts, tax refund) at the **smallest debt** until it's gone.
4. Once paid off, take the amount you were paying on that debt and **roll it** into the next smallest balance.
5. Repeat until you're debt-free.

This method doesn't just free your money—it frees your **mindset**. You feel like you're finally winning.

🧠 Why It Works (Psychology Over Math)

Critics say the Snowball Method isn't "mathematically efficient" because you might pay more in interest than the Avalanche Method.

But the truth is: **most people don't quit their debt elimination process because the math is wrong. They quit because the progress feels invisible.**

The Snowball Method works because:

- It gives you an early **emotional win**
- You see real progress fast
- You build **trust in yourself**
- You create momentum that's hard to stop

💡 *"It's not about the biggest savings. It's about the biggest shift in mindset."*

🧠 Case Study #1: Angela's $12,000 Snowball

Angela is a single mom who works as a nursing assistant. Let's first look at her revenue and expenses, then what is left after.

Phase	Months	Net Income	Living Expenses	Available for Debt	Notes
1) Kickoff	1–2	**$3,000**	**$2,325**	**$675**	Extra shifts start; focus on Medical bill to finish in 2 months
2) Doubledown	3–9	**$3,300**	**$2,200**	**$1,100**	Overtime (+$300) and temporary cuts (–$125) to crush both cards by month 9
3) Cruiseout	10–22	**$3,000**	**$2,325**	**$675**	Overtime ends; steady payoff of car to month 22

Here's what her debts looked like:

Line	Debt	Balance	Interest Rate	Monthly Payment
1	Medical Bill	$450	0%	$50
2	Credit Card A	$1,200	18.99%	$75
3	Credit Card B	$3,800	23.99%	$150
4	Car Loan	$6,500	7.5%	$225

Her debt minimums total = $500 (Medical $50 + CC A $75 + CC B $150 + Car $225).

What is the "extra" amount available after all minimum on debts ($500) have been paid?:

- Kick-off (month 1-2) extra is = **$175** ($675 – $500)

- Doubledown (month 3-9) extra is = **$600** ($1,100 – $500)
- Cruiseout (month 10-22) extra is = **$175** ($675 – $500)

Phase	Focus Debt	Effective Monthly Payment to Focus	Other Debts (paid at minimums)
1) Months 1–2	**Medical $450 @0%**	**$225** ($50 min + $175 extra) → **paid in 2 months**	CC A $75, CC B $150, Car $225
2a) Months 3–4*	**Credit Card A $1,200 @18.99%**	**$725** ($75 min + $50 (from Medical) + **$600 extra**) → **paid by month 4***	CC B $150, Car $225
2b) Months 5–9	**Credit Card B $3,800 @23.99%**	**$875** ($150 min + $125 (rolled from Medical + CC A) + **$600 extra**) → **both cards done by month 9**	Car $225
3) Months 10–22	**Car Loan $6,500 @7.5%**	**$675** ($225 min + $275 rolled from cards + **$175 extra**) → **paid by month 22**	—

CC A finishes around* ***month 4* *once Phase2 firepower hits; then its rolled amount joins CC B.*

Instead of focusing on the high-interest credit card first, she tackled her **$450 medical bill**. It took her **two months** to pay it off with extra shifts and budget cuts.

With that victory under her belt, she rolled the $50 she had been paying on the medical bill into Credit Card A.

By month 9, she had paid off both credit cards.

By month 22, she was completely debt-free—including the car loan.

Summary in numbers:

Phase 1 gives enough lift to clear the **$450 medical bill in 2 months** without starving other minimums.

Phase 2's temporary **$1,100/month debt budget** (overtime + cuts) is what makes **both cards gone by month 9** realistic **with interest included**.

Dropping back to **$675/month** in Phase 3 still finishes the **car by month 22** thanks to the rolled $275 (old minimums) plus the steady $175 extra.

> *"Each time I paid something off, I felt like I was walking a little taller. It gave me strength I didn't know I had."*

🧠 Case Study #2: Pierre & Lisette's Debt Snowball as a Couple

Pierre and Lisette are a couple with three kids. They were juggling, they felt stuck—barely making payments and constantly arguing about money.

Household Income & Expenses

Item	Monthly Amount
Net Household Income (Pierre + Lisette)	**$4,200**
Living Expenses (housing, food, utilities, kids, transport, etc.)	**$3,200**
Cash Flow Available for Debt	**$1,000**

☞ They were "barely making payments," they decided to cut dining out and Lisette pushed for a system with Shopunlocked.

$1,000/month is realistic for a family of five once they free up spending and add some freelance income.

Debt	Balance	Interest Rate	Monthly Payment
Store Credit Card	$900	24.99%	$65
Cell Phone Plan	$1,400	0% (financing)	$100
Furniture Loan	$2,300	19.99%	$110
Personal Loan	$5,000	13.5%	$160

Minimum Debt Payments

- Store Credit Card = **$65**
- Cell Phone = **$100**
- Furniture Loan = **$110**
- Personal Loan = **$160**
- **Total minimums = $435**

With **$1,000/month cash flow**, they have **$565 extra** to snowball.

Phase	Debt Focus	Balance	Min + Rolled	Extra Added	Total Payment to Focus	Months
1	Store Credit Card ($900)	$900	$65	+$565	**$630/mo**	**≈ 2 months**
2	Cell Phone Plan ($1,400)	$1,400	$100 + 65	+$565	**$730/mo**	**≈ 2 months**
3	Furniture Loan ($2,300)	$2,300	$110 + 165	+$565	**$840/mo**	**≈ 3 months**

4	Personal Loan ($5,000)	$5,000	$160 + 275	+$565	**$1,000/mo**	**≈ 11 months**

⏱️ Timeline Milestones

- **Month 2** → Store card gone 🎉
- **Month 4** → Cell phone paid off
- **Month 7** → Furniture loan gone
- **Month 18** → Personal loan gone → **Debt-free!**

They celebrated together, felt reconnected, and doubled down.

Within **18 months**, they had paid off everything.

> *"Paying off that first card saved our budget—but also saved our peace."*

Self-Check: Start Your Snowball

Purpose: Build your personal payoff plan using the Snowball Method.

Steps:

1. List all your debts from **smallest to largest balance**.
2. Write down your **minimum payment** for each.
3. Choose the first target (smallest).
4. Decide how much **extra** you can pay monthly.

5. Track each victory and **roll the payment** into the next.

🗒️ Example:

Debt	Balance	Min. Payment	Paid Off?
Credit Card A	$520	$45	☑ Month 2
Furniture Loan	$1,100	$85	⌛ Active
Car Loan	$4,800	$220	✕

🔄 Rewire Your Story

If you've ever told yourself:

> *"It's going to take too long... I might as well give up."*

Say this instead:

> *"I don't need to finish today. I just need to win today's round. Progress stacks. Confidence builds. I will keep going."*

💬 Written just for you

> *"Each debt you pay off is one less hand in your pocket—and one more brick in your freedom."*

8.4 The Avalanche Method: The Smartest Math Wins

☑ What Is the Avalanche Method?

The **Avalanche Method** is a strategic approach to paying off debt by targeting the **highest-interest debt first**, not the smallest balance.

Why? Because over time, the highest-interest debts **cost you the most money**.

Just like a real avalanche that starts high and gathers power as it drops, this method helps you **reduce your interest payments first**, so your money goes farther—faster.

🔧 How the Avalanche Method Works (Step-by-Step)

1. **List all your debts** from highest to lowest **interest rate**, regardless of balance.
2. **Make minimum payments** on all debts—except the one with the **highest APR**.
3. Throw **everything extra** you can at that high-interest debt until it's gone.
4. Once paid off, **roll that payment** into the next highest-interest debt.
5. Repeat until you're debt-free.

💡 *The Avalanche Method isn't just about discipline—it's about efficiency. You pay less in interest and get out faster.*

🧠 Why It Works (Math Over Emotion)

If the **Snowball Method** is about momentum and motivation, the **Avalanche Method** is about precision and **maximum financial impact**.

You might not get the quick win of paying off a small debt right away, but:

- You'll pay less in total interest
- You'll get out of debt **sooner** if you stay consistent
- You avoid wasting money on high-cost balances that grow faster

📊 *It's the difference between wiping out weeds and pulling the roots. The Avalanche Method hits what's hurting you the most.*

🧠 Case Study #1: Marc's $20,000 Avalanche Strategy

Marc is 34, a freelance graphic designer with inconsistent income.

Step 1) Household Budget & Cash Flow

Item	Amount
Net household income	**$4,000**
Fixed expenses (rent 1,500; utilities 250; insurance 200; transport 250; childcare/school 350)	**$2,550**
Variable expenses (groceries 500; dining 120; subscriptions 120; misc 100)	**$840**
Total living expenses	**$3,390**
Cash flow available for debt	**$610**

We'll keep the "debt budget" steady at **$610/mo**. "Debt budget" means the "extra" amount available each month after all expenses (cash flow). This amount is what makes the debt elimination process work, whether you are using the Avalanche method or the Snowball method.

Step 2) Avalanche Order = Highest APR first

Let's rearrange the table

Priority	Debt	Balance	APR	Min. Payment
#1	Store Credit Card	$900	24.99%	$65
#2	Furniture Loan	$2,300	19.99%	$110
#3	Personal Loan	$5,000	13.5%	$160
#4	Cell Phone Plan (0% financing)	$1,400	0%	$100
	Total minimums			$435

This is the way to understand the process we are about to apply with the Avalanche method:

1. While focusing on debt **#1 Store Card**, we keep paying **minimums on all other debts** and use our cash flow (any extra money left after all expenses) to pay on the debt we are focusing on (exampe for now: #1 store card).
2. With a $610 monthly debt budget (monthly cash flow / "monthly extra") shown in **step 1** and $435 in total minimums to be paid monthly shown in **step 2**, extra = **$175 per month ($610-$435).**
3. So, while Store Card is the focus for now: **Store card gets $65** (regular minimum monthly payment) + **$175** (debt budget)= **$240/mo**; other debt get their regular minimum payments as usual.

Let's Avalanche the first debt only for now (Store Credit Card)

Phase 1: Payment plan this phase (each month):

- Store Card: **$240**
- Cell: **$100**
- Furniture: **$110**
- Personal: **$160**
- **Total monthly outflow = $610**

Payoff Table – Store Credit Card (24.99% APR, starting balance $900)

Mo.	Start Balance	Interest	Payment to Store Card	Principal Paid	End Balance
1	$900.00	$18.74	**$240.00**	$221.26	$678.74
2	$678.74	$14.13	**$240.00**	$225.87	$452.87
3	$452.87	$9.43	**$240.00**	$230.57	$222.30
4	$222.30	$4.63	**$226.93**	$222.30	**$0.00**

Result: Store card paid in **4 months.**
Total interest paid on this debt: $46.93.

Let's Avalanche the second debt (Furniture Loan, 19.99% APR)

Starting balance: $2,300
Min. payment: $110
Amount rollover from paid off Store Card: +$240
New monthly payment to Furniture Loan: $350 ($110 regular min + rollover from debt 1 paid off)

NB: (Other debts stay at minimums: Cell $100, Personal $160)
Total debt budget remains $610/mo

Phase 2: Payoff Table – Furniture Loan

Mo.	Start Balance	Interest	Payment to Furniture	Principal Paid	End Balance
1	$2,300.00	$38.33	**$350.00**	$311.67	$1,988.33
2	$1,988.33	$33.15	**$350.00**	$316.85	$1,671.48
3	$1,671.48	$27.87	**$350.00**	$322.13	$1,349.35
4	$1,349.35	$22.49	**$350.00**	$327.51	$1,021.84
5	$1,021.84	$17.03	**$350.00**	$332.97	$688.87
6	$688.87	$11.48	**$350.00**	$338.52	$350.35
7	$350.35	$5.83	**$356.18**	$350.35	**$0.00**

Result: Furniture Loan paid in **7 months.**
Total interest paid on this debt: $156.18

Let's Avalanche the third debt (Personal Loan, 13.5% APR)

Starting balance: $5,000
Min. payment: $160
Rolled over from paid off Store card + Furniture: +$350
New monthly payment to Personal Loan: $510 ($160 regular min + rollover from debt 1 & 2 paid off)
(Meanwhile, Cell Phone Plan keeps its $100 minimum.)
Total monthly debt budget still = $610

Phase 3: Payoff Table – Personal Loan

Mo.	Start Balance	Interest	Payment to Personal	Principal Paid	End Balance
1	$5,000.00	$56.25	**$510.00**	$453.75	$4,546.25
2	$4,546.25	$51.14	**$510.00**	$458.86	$4,087.39
3	$4,087.39	$45.98	**$510.00**	$464.02	$3,623.37
4	$3,623.37	$40.77	**$510.00**	$469.23	$3,154.14
5	$3,154.14	$35.52	**$510.00**	$474.48	$2,679.66
6	$2,679.66	$30.15	**$510.00**	$479.85	$2,199.81
7	$2,199.81	$24.75	**$510.00**	$485.25	$1,714.56
8	$1,714.56	$19.32	**$510.00**	$490.68	$1,223.88
9	$1,223.88	$13.79	**$510.00**	$496.21	$727.67
10	$727.67	$8.19	**$510.00**	$501.81	$225.86
11	$225.86	$2.54	**$228.40**	$225.86	**$0.00**

Result: Personal Loan paid in **11 months.**
Total interest paid on this debt: $328.40

Let's Avalanche the fourth debt (Cell Phone Plan, 0% APR)

Starting balance: $1,400
Min. payment: $100
Rolled over from all previous debts: +$510
New monthly payment: $610
(No interest since 0% financing.)

Phase 4: Payoff Table – Cell Phone Plan

Mo.	Start Balance	Interest	Payment	Principal Paid	End Balance
1	$1,400.00	$0.00	**$610.00**	$610.00	$790.00
2	$790.00	$0.00	**$610.00**	$610.00	$180.00
3	$180.00	$0.00	**$180.00**	$180.00	**$0.00**

Result: Cell Phone paid in **3 months.**
Total interest paid: $0 ☑

🎉 Final Results – Avalanche Method (Pierre & Lisette)

- **Store Credit Card:** 4 months paid off
- **Furniture Loan:** 7 months paid off
- **Personal Loan:** 11 months paid off
- **Cell Phone Plan:** 3 months paid off

Total = 25 months to debt freedom (≈ 2 years, 1 month)
Total interest paid: ~$531.51

> *"It wasn't exciting in the beginning, but once I saw how fast the interest stopped piling up, I got hooked."*

> ⚖ *Compared to the* **Snowball method**, *the Avalanche method might take a little longer to be debt free, but the Avalanche method* **saves you money in interest.**

Let's quickly compare the two methods with numbers, using **Pierre & Lisette's case study**

Metric	Snowball Method	Avalanche Method
Strategy Focus	**Smallest balance first**	**Highest interest rate first**
First Debt Paid	Store Card ($900)	Store Card ($900)
Final Debt Paid	Personal Loan ($5,000)	Cell Phone Plan ($1,400, 0%)
Total Time to Debt-Free	**18 months**	**25 months**
Total Interest Paid	**~ $1,250**	**~ $532**
Psychological Benefit	Quick wins, strong motivation	Slower visible progress
Financial Benefit	Faster overall timeline	Saves ~ **$718** in interest

☑ **Snowball**: Best for momentum, emotional wins, faster freedom.
☑ **Avalanche**: Best for minimizing total interest paid, though it takes longer.

🧠 Case Study #2: Judith's Avalanche vs. Snowball Dilemma

Judith, a high school teacher in Florida, was choosing between the two methods.

Step 1 – Income, Expenses, and Cash Flow

Judith's Monthly Budget

Item	Amount
Net Income (teacher salary)	**$3,800**
Fixed expenses (rent 1,300; utilities 250; insurance 200; transport 300; phone/internet 120)	**$2,170**
Variable expenses (groceries 500; personal 230; misc 210)	**$940**
Total Living Expenses	**$3,110**
Cash Flow Available for Debt	**$690**

Her debts:

Debt	Balance	Interest Rate	Monthly Payment
Store Card	$650	19.99%	$45
Credit Card	$2,800	**25.99%**	$90
Student Loan	$9,000	6.5%	$150

Minimum Debt Payments

- Store Card = $45
- Credit Card = $90
- Student Loan = $150
- **Total minimums = $285**

So Judith can apply an **extra $405/month** ($690 – $285) toward whichever debt she focuses on.

📊 Step 2 – Snowball vs Avalanche dilemma

Metric	Snowball Method	Avalanche Method
Strategy Focus	Smallest balance first	Highest interest rate first
First Debt Paid	Store Card ($650)	Credit Card ($2,800 @ 25.99%)
Total Time to Debt-Free	~ **46 months** (3 yrs 10 mo)	~ **40 months** (3 yrs 4 mo)
Total Interest Paid	~ **$6,800**	~ **$4,900**
Savings	—	**≈ $1,900 less interest**
Psychological Benefit	Fast win in ~2 months (store card gone)	Slow start, but major financial savings
Judith's Choice	Initially Snowball (for quick relief)	Switched to Avalanche after realizing credit card cost

She wanted to do Snowball at first because **knocking out the store card fast felt satisfying.**

But after, she realized that her **25.99% credit card** would cost her additional interest if she left it untouched.

☑ Key Takeaway

Snowball: would have given Judith a quick boost but cost her **6 months longer** and **~$1,900 more in interest**.

Avalanche: was slower emotionally but smarter mathematically — she paid less interest, finished faster, and gained peace of mind.

> *"I chose math over feelings—and now I'm feeling really good about it."*

🟩 Self-Check: Choose the method that works for YOU

Purpose: Build a debt attack plan based on chosen method.

Steps:

1. List all your debts with **interest rates and balances**.
2. Rank them according to the method chosen.
3. Highlight your first debt – according to the method you have chosen
4. Figure out how much **extra** you can pay toward it each month. You need a budget. You need to know your monthly cash flow (see book: "Start with this")
5. Make a plan to **roll payments** down as each debt is eliminated.

🔄 Rewire Your Story

If you've thought:

> *"This is too slow. I need fast wins to stay motivated."*

Try reframing it as:

> *"I'm playing the long game. Every dollar I save in interest is one more I keep for my future."*

Not every win feels emotional—but some wins are **more powerful in the long run.**

💬 Written just for you

> *"The Avalanche Method doesn't move fast at first—but it clears the path for everything after."*

📌 Chapter Summary: What You've Conquered

Sometimes the smartest move isn't the fastest—it's the one that frees you forever.

- **The Avalanche Method attacks your most expensive debt first.**
  You save the most money by eliminating high-interest accounts early.
- **It's not always about the smallest balance**—it's about the biggest threat.
- **Every dollar of interest you don't pay is a dollar you get to keep.**
  And those dollars add up.
- **This method requires patience**—but it also delivers the fastest financial freedom if you stay consistent.

🌟 Next Step

In Chapter 9, we begin putting it all together: your real numbers, your debt lineup, and your personal strategy. We'll build your first battle plan—with numbers you understand and decisions you'll own.

◇ PART 2 – DO IT

YOUR STEP-BY-STEP WORKBOOK - DO IT STRATEGIZE, TRACK, AND CRUSH YOUR DEBT

"This isn't just about numbers. It's about reclaiming your choices, your peace, and your life."

This page is left intentionally blank

CHAPTER 9

Action time: your debt-free game plan

> *"You don't need a financial degree, or a rich uncle. You need a pencil, some truth, and the will to stick to the plan."*

☑ 9.1– The Power of Facing It All

"I thought ignoring my debt meant it would bother me less. Turns out, it only gave it more power."

Let me introduce you to Allan. He avoided his bank app for three straight months. He paid the minimum on his cards, yes—but he never looked at the balances. He told himself, *"I'll deal with it when I make more."*

Then one day, an unexpected overdraft triggered a cascade of bounced payments. The stress made him feel sick. And that's when he realized:

"The scariest part wasn't the number—it was not knowing the number."

That's what this chapter is about: **knowing.**

Not to shame you. But to **take the keys back from the fear that's been driving your financial life.**

📌 Getting Approved: What You'll Need & Who You'll Talk To

In order to apply any of the strategies (Avalanche / Snowball) we have discussed previously in this book, you need to choose your weapon, your tool (0% credit card, personal loan, heloc, etc)

Here are a few tools and how you can get access to them:

🏛 1. Personal Loan

When to use: Debt consolidation, emergency expenses, home repairs, etc.

Who to talk to:

- Bank or credit union loan officer
- Online lender

Documents you'll need:

- Government-issued ID
- Proof of income (pay stubs, W-2s, tax returns)
- Employment verification
- Recent bank statements
- Credit report (they'll pull it)

Typical credit score needed:

- ✅ **Excellent (740+):** Best interest rates (5%–8%)
- ⚠️ **Good (670–739):** Approved with higher interest rates (9%–16%)
- ❌ **Fair or Poor (<670):** Higher interest rates or co-signer required

🔁 2. Personal Line of Credit (Unsecured LOC)

When to use: Flexible borrowing for business needs, emergencies, or strategic debt payoff

Who to talk to:

- Your personal banker at a traditional bank or credit union
- Business banker if for self-employed/sole proprietors

Documents you'll need:

- Government-issued ID
- Proof of consistent income
- Employment verification
- Tax returns (especially if self-employed)
- Bank statements
- Credit report

Typical credit score needed:

- ☑ **720+** best terms
- ⚠ **680–719** moderate approval
- ✕ **Below 680** may require collateral or be denied

💡 *Tip: Credit unions tend to offer more lenient underwriting than big banks.*

🔁 3. Personal Line of Credit (Unsecured LOC)

When to use: Flexible borrowing for business needs, emergencies, or strategic debt payoff

Who to talk to:

- Your personal banker at a traditional bank or credit union
- Business banker if for self-employed/sole proprietors

Documents you'll need:

- Government-issued ID
- Proof of consistent income
- Employment verification
- Tax returns (especially if self-employed)
- Bank statements
- Credit report

Typical credit score needed:

- ☑ **720+** best terms
- ⚠ **680–719** moderate approval
- ❌ **Below 680** may require collateral or be denied

💡 *Tip: Credit unions tend to offer more lenient underwriting than big banks.*

🏠 4. Home Equity Line of Credit (HELOC)

When to use: Debt consolidation, home renovations, or emergency cushion

Who to talk to:

- Mortgage loan officer at your current bank or lender
- Home lending department at a credit union or local community bank

Documents you'll need:

- Government-issued ID
- Recent mortgage statement
- Proof of homeownership (deed/title)
- Proof of income
- Tax returns (2 years)
- Home appraisal (often required)
- Homeowners insurance
- Credit report

Typical credit score needed:

- ☑ **700+** best rates
- ⚠ **660–699** approved with higher rates
- ✖ **Below 660** may be denied or limited in credit

💡 *You usually need **at least 15–20% equity** in your home to qualify.*

🏠💳 5. First-Lien HELOC

When to use: Advanced mortgage strategy for rapid debt payoff (see later in this book); replaces traditional mortgage

Who to talk to:

- Specialized lender that offers **first-position HELOCs** (not all banks do)
- Mortgage brokers with HELOC expertise
- Credit unions and Fintechs specializing in flexible lending (e.g., Figure, First Lien HELOC lenders)

Documents you'll need:

- Same as standard HELOC, plus:
    - Detailed monthly budget
    - Proof of strong, consistent cash flow
    - Willingness to refinance entire mortgage
    - Home appraisal required

- Deed transfer or title work for lien positioning

Typical credit score needed:

- ☑ **740+** strongly preferred
- ⚠ **700–739** considered with strong income and equity
- ❌ **Below 700** rarely approved

⚠ *This product is* ***not for beginners****. You must understand cash flow, banking discipline, and how to avoid misusing revolving credit.*

💳 6. Credit Card (Low Interest or Rewards)

How to use: Day-to-day spending, building credit, balance transfers

Who to talk to:

- Online applications (Amex, Discover, Capital One, etc.).

  Great deal☞ copy/paste into your browser:

  https://i.capitalone.com/GsVEPCNxs

- In-branch representative at your bank or credit union

Documents you'll need:

- Government-issued ID
- Proof of income (sometimes optional)
- Social Security number

- Employment info

Typical credit score needed:

- ☑ **Excellent (740+):** Access to 0% APR promos, top-tier rewards, lowest ongoing rates
- ⚠ **Good (700–739):** May qualify for good cards, but watch out for higher APR
- ✕ **Below 700:** Likely to get high-interest or secured cards

☑ Final Advice

> 💬 *"Never walk into a loan meeting blind. Know your credit score, your budget, and your reason for borrowing before you ever fill out a form."*

📌 Using Your Tool: Step by Step

📌 Using a 0% Balance Transfer Credit Card

Once you've been approved, the next step is knowing how to actually use the tool to make your debt strategy work. For example, let's go back to Judith, the teacher from Florida. She chose the Avalanche Method and decided to apply for a 0% balance transfer credit card. Here's how she used it:

Transfer the high-interest debt first – Judith moved her $2,800 credit card (25.99% interest) onto the new 0%

card. This immediately stopped the expensive interest charges that were costing her $1,200+ per year.

Keep paying the same amount – Even though her new minimum payment was much lower, Judith kept paying the $495 per month she had already budgeted. With no interest piling up, every dollar went straight to reducing the balance.

Stick to the payoff window – Because the 0% offer lasted 18 months, Judith's goal was to finish that balance before the promo ended. She tracked progress monthly to stay on schedule.

Then roll the payment forward – Once the credit card was gone, she applied the freed-up $495 each month to her student loan, shrinking her timeline even more.

By using the right tool the right way, Judith didn't just shuffle debt around—she used it as a bridge to speed up her Avalanche plan, saving almost $2,000 in interest and cutting six months off her journey.

📌 Using a Personal Loan

Now consider Angela, the single mom with $12,000 of debt. Instead of juggling four different payments—medical bill, two credit cards, and a car loan—she could have applied for a personal loan at 9% interest. With approval, the bank would pay off her credit cards and medical bill in one shot. Instead of paying multiple minimums (and getting crushed by 24% credit card interest), Angela would now have one fixed monthly payment that fits her budget. This gave her a clear end date, lower interest costs, and less stress from managing different due dates.

📌 Using a HELOC (Home Equity Line of Credit)

Finally, picture Pierre & Lisette, the couple with three kids and $9,600 of debt spread across a store card, cell phone plan, furniture loan, and personal loan. Because they owned a home with equity, they could open a HELOC at 6% interest. They borrowed just enough from the HELOC to pay off all their higher-interest debts (some at 20%+). Their debts were now consolidated into one line of credit with a much lower interest rate. They set strict rules: keep making the same $1,000 a month they had budgeted for debt and never use the HELOC for new spending. By doing this, they kept the discipline of their Snowball plan but saved hundreds in interest and cut their payoff time dramatically.

☑ Summary:

- The 0% card is like a shield against high-interest.
- The personal loan is like a reset button, replacing chaos with structure.
- The HELOC is like a lever, turning home equity into a lower-cost way to crush debt.

📌 What You've Learned So Far

"The most dangerous thing about money isn't how much you have. It's how little you're taught to understand it."

🔎 Key Takeaways

- Financial language is a barrier by design. But you can learn it—and learning it makes you unshakable.
- Knowing the difference between APR and APY helps you avoid traps.
- Amortization, balance transfers, 0% APR deals—all have emotional and financial risks when misunderstood.
- Budgeting gets smarter when you understand fixed vs. variable expenses.
- An emergency fund gives you breathing room and power.
- Your debt payoff method should fit *your brain*, not just the math.

💬 *"When you speak money fluently, no one can sell you fear disguised as opportunity."*

🔍 Why You Can't Skip This Step

Budgeting without a full debt inventory is like trying to cook a meal without knowing what ingredients you have. You'll end up frustrated, wasteful, and going in circles.

This chapter is where you:

- List all your debts
- Name what you owe and to whom
- Get clear on **what it's costing you monthly and emotionally**

No more guessing. No more "around $200" or "I think it's almost paid off." Just **facts.**

🧠 9.2– Worksheet: My Current Debt Snapshot

This is your **financial mirror**. It's not to judge you—it's to give you a clear reflection so you can start changing what you see.

Debt Type	Balance	Interest Rate (APR)	Minimum Payment	Years in Debt
Credit Card A	$3,200	24.99%	$95	2 years
Car Loan	$6,000	8.0%	$240	1.5 years
Personal Loan	$4,500	12.5%	$160	3 years
Student Loan	$7,800	6.5%	$120	5 years

Use the below worksheet—or draw it in your notebook. What matters is that **you get it all out of your head and onto paper.**

Here is a blank one (feel free to write in the book)

Debt Type	Balance	Interest Rate (APR)	Minimum Payment	Years in Debt

🔄 Rewire Your Story

If your brain has been whispering:

> *"Don't look—it's too depressing."*

Say instead:

> *"My debt is not my identity. These are just numbers. I get to decide what happens next."*

Every time you face the facts, you begin the healing. You build **clarity, discipline, and power**.

☑ 9.3– What I Really Have Left Each Month

Knowing what you owe is only half the battle. The other half is knowing what you actually **have left**—after all your bills and obligations are paid.

This isn't about budgeting perfection. It's about honest awareness.

Use this simple formula:

Income – Expenses = Reality
Let's take an example.

Category	Amount
Total Monthly Income	$3,600
Rent	$1,200
Utilities	$250
Food	$500
Transportation	$300
Debt Payments	$700
Subscriptions, Misc.	$200
Left Over = Cash Flow	**$450**

Now ask:

> *"Is this enough to attack my smallest debt? Where could I cut without hurting myself?"*

You need this number because **this is the fuel** you'll use to fire up your Snowball or Avalanche.

▧ Self-Check: Debt Timeline Vision

Purpose: Visualize your progress. Make it real. Stay motivated.

Steps:

1. Draw a **12-month calendar** in your journal or download a printable.
2. Write your **starting total debt** at the top.
3. Create a rough plan: what you hope your debt balance will be each month.

4. Assign a **milestone** to each quarter:
   - "Paid off Credit Card A"
   - "Cut $100 in flexible spending"
   - "Emergency fund hits $500"
   - "Zero balance on car loan"

💡 *Visual progress helps your brain feel safe. It replaces fear with focus.*

EXAMPLE – Table format

📋 Debt Snapshot Worksheet – Judith's Plan (Avalanche Method)

Assumptions

- Credit card: $5,200 at 28.5% APR, minimum ≈ 3% (lower $35)
- Store card: $1,650 at 24.99% APR, minimum ≈ 3% (lower $25)

- Student loan: $5,600 at 6.5% APR, minimum $75
- Total monthly payment: $690 (minimum on all + excess toward the highest rate)

Starting Debt Total: $12,450

Month	Beg. Bal	Payment	Interest	Capital	Expected Balance
1	12 450,00	690,00	188,19	501,81	11 948,19
2	11 948,19	690,00	177,14	512,86	11 435,34
3	11 435,34	690,00	165,83	524,17	10 911,17
4	10 911,17	690,00	154,26	535,74	10 375,43
5	10 375,43	690,00	142,41	547,59	9 827,84
6	9 827,84	690,00	130,28	559,72	9 268,12
7	9 268,12	690,00	117,85	572,15	8 696,00
8	8 696,00	690,00	105,11	584,89	8 111,11
9	8 111,11	690,00	92,04	597,96	7 513,15
10	7 513,15	690,00	78,62	611,38	6 901,77
11	6 901,77	690,00	64,83	625,17	6 276,60
12	6 276,60	690,00	52,22	637,78	5 639,78

☑ Year 1 Review

- Total paid: $8,280
- Interest paid ≈ $1,469.78
- Principal repaid ≈ $6,810.22
- Remaining balance ≈ $5,639.78 (vs. $12,450 initially)
- Avalanche Steps (with these rates):
    - Credit card (28.5%) paid off in month 11

- Store card (24.99%) ≈ month 13 (just after year 1)
- Student loan (6.5%) ≈ month 21

Use the next page to insert your own numbers:

📋 Debt Snapshot Worksheet – 12-Month Plan

Starting Debt Total: $______________

Month	Starting Balance	Planned Payment	Planned Balance	☑ Milestone / Notes
1	$______	$______	$______	☐ ________________
2	$______	$______	$______	☐ ________________
3	$______	$______	$______	☐ ________________
4	$______	$______	$______	☐ ________________
5	$______	$______	$______	☐ ________________
6	$______	$______	$______	☐ ________________
7	$______	$______	$______	☐ ________________
8	$______	$______	$______	☐ ________________

9	$____	$_____	$_____	☐ ______________
10	$_____	$_____	$_____	☐ ______________
11	$_____	$_____	$_____	☐ ______________
12	$_____	$_____	$_____	☐ ______________

☑ 9.4– Why This Chapter Is the Turning Point

It might not feel exciting to list out numbers. It might even feel draining.
But this chapter—this quiet act of telling the truth—is often where the biggest breakthroughs begin.

You don't need more hustle.
You need more **visibility.**

Once you have the facts, your emotions can **settle**. Your plan can **start**. And your belief in a different future can finally feel **real**.

💬 Written just for you

> *"Clarity is kindness. The truth doesn't hurt you—it heals you."*

In Chapter 12 we'll see how this works in real life

📌 Chapter Summary: What You've Conquered

> *When you name the numbers, you name the path forward.*

- **Avoidance increases anxiety.** Facing the facts—even if they're messy—calms the chaos.
- **Debt is just data.** Shame fades when you start using your brain instead of just your fear.
- **Inventory reveals opportunity.** You can't solve what you haven't named.
- **Tracking your "leftover money" gives you control.** It's the seed of your strategy.
- **Visualization fuels belief.** A 12-month timeline helps your brain shift from hopeless to hopeful.

✸ Next Step

You've laid the foundation. Now we're moving from learning into **doing**.

In Chapter 10, we'll begin building your personalized debt strategy—using either the Snowball or Avalanche method. You'll know exactly where your focus should go first, and why.

This page is left intentionally blank

CHAPTER 10

Set Your Goals and Pick Your Weapon

When Clarity Meets Commitment

☑ 10.1– Before You Pay Off a Dime, Know What You're Fighting For

> *"If you aim at nothing, you'll hit it every time."*
> *– Zig Ziglar*

Sophia was tired of seeing $5 here, $10 there disappear from her account like ghosts. She'd tried throwing "extra" money at her credit card before—but it never stuck. She'd try for a month, then stop. Try again. Stop.

One day, she sat down and wrote this:

"I want to pay off $3,000 in 9 months, without borrowing again. I'll use my Uber Eats side hustle for extra payments."

That one sentence? It changed everything.

That's called a **SMART Goal**—and it's the difference between random effort and real results.

🔧 What Makes a Goal SMART?

S.M.A.R.T is an acronym:

- **S**pecific – Say *what* debt, *how much*, *by when*
- **M**easurable – You can track progress over time
- **A**chievable – Within your income limits, not fantasy
- **R**elevant – Connects to your real life (not someone else's dream)
- **T**ime-bound – Has a start and end date

Let's rewrite Sophia's:

❌ "I want to get out of debt this year."
☑ "I will pay off my $3,000 credit card balance in 9 months by making $333 monthly payments from my side hustle and cutting takeout spending."

Big difference, right?

▧ Self-Check: SMART Goal Builder

Purpose: Clarify exactly what you're trying to do.

Steps:

1. Pick one debt to focus on first.
2. Write the total balance.
3. Choose a reasonable time frame.

4. Break the goal into monthly payments.
5. Identify where that payment will come from.

Example:

- Debt: $1,800 car loan
- Time: 6 months
- Monthly payment: $300
- Source: Cut subscriptions + freelance income

💡 *Now you have a weapon with a target, not just a good intention.*

Let's do an example with your own numbers here:

Pick one debt to focus on first.	
Write the total balance	
Choose a reasonable time frame.	
Break the goal into monthly payments (Line 2 above divided by 12)	
Identify where that payment will come from.	

☑ 10.2– Snowball vs. Avalanche: Choose Your Attack Style

Now that you've listed your debts (previous chapters) and set a goal, let's talk **strategy**.

We've defined in previous chapters the two famous debt payoff methods:

🔨 The Snowball Method

- **Start with**: The smallest debt balance.
- **Why it works**: You get quick wins that keep you motivated.
- **Psychology**: Builds confidence fast—perfect for emotional momentum.

🎯 Example:

- Credit Card A: $300 → done in 1 month.
- Credit Card B: $1,200 → next target.
- Car Loan: $5,800 → later, but doable.

Each paid-off account gives you a **rush**—and that's powerful.

🔬 The Avalanche Method

- **Start with**: The highest interest rate, regardless of balance.
- **Why it works**: You pay less in total interest over time.
- **Psychology**: Requires patience, but saves the most money.

🎯 Example:

- Credit Card C: $2,000 at 27.99% → hits first
- Car Loan: $4,000 at 7% → hits last

If you like **math and logic**, Avalanche is your method.
If you need **emotional wins fast**, choose Snowball.

🧠 10.3– Case Study: Which One Helped More?

Let's look at two friends: Janelle and Erika.

- Both had $5,000 in total debt.
- Both paid $500/month.

Janelle used **Avalanche**

- Erika used **Snowball**
- Details of the debts:

    1. $1,200 at 28.99%
    2. $800 at 24.99%
    3. $1,400 at 19.99%
    4. $600 at 14.99%
    5. $1,000 at 9.99%

Method	Months to Pay Off	Total Paid	Interest Paid
Avalanche (highest rate first)	**11 months**	**$6,200**	**$1,200**
Snowball (smallest balance first)	**12 months**	**$6,350**	**$1,350**

The cost difference? $150.

But guess what?

Erika stayed consistent and finished. Janelle paused twice and almost quit.

The best method? **The one you'll stick to.**

🔄 **Rewire Your Story**

If your brain says:

> "I've never stuck to a plan before. Why bother?"

You say:

> *"I don't have to be perfect—I just have to keep going. Every payment is a proof of commitment."*

Consistency beats intensity every time. This chapter is about creating a **structure that supports your strength—not your shame.**

🧠 10.4– The Low Balance Panic – When Doing the Right Thing *Feels* Wrong

Let's talk about the shock that hits when you **finally do the smart thing**—and your bank account looks... scary.

"Why does it feel like I'm still broke—even when I'm finally doing the right thing?"

You're finally applying your debt plan. You're not overspending.
You're following your budget.
You made your extra debt payment.

You've:

- Skipped takeout.

- Said no to overspending.

But then you open your bank app...
and see **$24.79.**

Instant panic.

You start thinking things like:

- *"This can't be right."*
- *"I need a cushion!"*
- *"Maybe I shouldn't have paid extra this month..."*
- *"Did I just mess up?"*
- *"What if something comes up?"*
- *"This doesn't feel safe..."*

That fear? It's real. And **normal**.

You're not alone.

🧠 Why We Panic at a Low Bank Balance (Even When It's Planned)

As humans, we're wired to **feel safe when we can see our resources**.
A full fridge. A full gas tank. A full bank account.

It's a **visual form of control**.

So when your checking account dips low—even for a good reason—your brain sometimes interprets it as **danger**, not progress.

This is especially true if you:

- Grew up with financial instability
- Are the provider in your family
- Have experienced "money disappearing overnight"

It's a trauma response, not a financial mistake.

A low balance triggers the **fight or flight** center in your brain.

But this is not a threat—it's **strategy in motion**.
And that's okay.

🔄 Rewire Your Story (Money Trauma Edition)

Tell yourself:

> *"This discomfort is growth. I'm not failing. I'm investing in freedom."*

> *"My bank account may be low—but my purpose is full."*

It's okay to feel uneasy. But don't undo your progress to soothe a false alarm.

🧭 The Mindset Shift: Progress Doesn't Always Feel Comfortable

Here's the truth you need to remind yourself of—daily if necessary:

Seeing a low balance is sometimes part of the plan.

It doesn't mean you're failing—it means you're *redirecting your money to where it matters.*

When you're paying off debt aggressively, your account **will dip low** for a few weeks or months.

That's not forever. That's **temporary intensity**.

It's like going to the gym: your muscles get sore before they get stronger.

Likewise, your finances feel "tight" before they get *free.*

✨ Repeat After Me:

✦ "This low balance is not a crisis. It's the proof that I'm actively changing my life."

✦ "I'm not broke—I'm building."

✦ "Every dollar I moved paid down debt. That money is working for me."

✦ "This feeling is temporary. Freedom is coming."

💡 Don't Shift the Shame

Some of us are so used to feeling shame about debt, that we just shift that shame to something else:

- "Now I feel bad about not having savings."
- "I feel exposed with just $50 in my account."

But guess what? That's **not productive.**
You're doing the hard thing. Don't punish yourself while doing it.

Instead, track how much debt you've paid this month. Focus on that number—not the short-term dip in your bank account.

That's your real progress.

☑ **Strategy Tip:**

If it helps your anxiety, keep a **small emergency buffer**—$100–$250—untouched, and still go hard on debt.
This gives your brain peace while your money works.

📱 LOW BALANCE ≠ FAILURE

A Gentle Reminder for When You're Doing the Right Thing

💡 **This Is Not a Crisis.**

Your low balance isn't a sign of failure.
It's proof that you're finally moving forward.

💪 **You're Not Broke—You're Building.**

✔ You made your debt payment.
✔ You paid your bills on time.
✔ You followed your plan.
✔ You didn't waste.
✔ You're in control.

🧠 **Calm the Panic.**

Your brain wants to see a "cushion" to feel safe.

But today, your safety is in the **discipline**, not the digits.

Remember This:

✔ You can rebuild your savings—debt-free.
✔ This is temporary.
✔ Shame doesn't help. Strategy does.

TIP: Peace + Progress = Power.

Written just for you

> *"You're not broke—you're building. Your balance is low because your priorities are high."*

Chapter Summary: What You've Conquered

Strategy kills chaos. Clarity kills fear.

- **SMART goals turn hope into action.** Don't wing it—write it down.
- **Snowball = fast wins. Avalanche = big savings.** Choose what matches your emotional and financial reality.
- **Panic is normal—but not proof you're failing.** Your low balance is temporary. Your freedom is coming.
- **Rewiring takes repetition.** Keep speaking power over panic.
- **This isn't about willpower—it's about structure.** When your system is strong, you don't need to be.

✹ Next Step

Ready to test your strategy?

Let's figure out your style, your traps, and how to stay on track for the long haul.

CHAPTER 11

Make the Plan Yours

Set Your Attack Plan

"There's no 'one-size-fits-all' to freedom. But there is one truth: Your plan must feel like yours—or you won't follow it."

☑ 11.1– The Week Lionel Took Control

✦ Lionel used to feel like his paycheck was already gone before it hit the bank.

Rent, food, minimum payments. Nothing left. Always behind.

Until one Friday night, something shifted.

Instead of scrolling on his phone, he sat with a notebook. He wrote:

- How much came in weekly
- What bills hit and when
- How much was left after bare minimum expenses

He realized he could take $60 that week and knock down part of a high-interest credit card.

He did it again next week.

He started winning weekly.
Now, Lionel doesn't budget monthly—he manages cash flow **weekly**.

And that's why he's no longer stuck.

🔍 The Power of Weekly Cash Flow Tracking

If you've been budgeting monthly and still falling behind, it's time to zoom in.

Weekly planning gives you real-time control. Monthly planning gives you strategy.

Here's how it works:

1. **Every Friday or Sunday**, list your income and bills due in the next 7 days.
2. Note what's fixed (like rent) vs. flexible (like takeout).
3. Identify any extra you can put toward debt **that week.**
4. Repeat, adjust, and win again.

When you treat every week like a chance to make progress, your momentum builds faster.

📋 Weekly Monitoring Worksheet

Week of: ______________________________

Category	**Planned ($)**	**Actual ($)**	**Difference ($)**	**Notes / Adjustments**
Income (take-home, side hustle)	______	______	______	______________
Fixed Expenses (rent, utilities, insurance)	______	______	______	______________
Variable Expenses (groceries, gas, dining)	______	______	______	______________
Debt Payments (minimums + extra)	______	______	______	______________
Savings (emergency fund, sinking funds)	______	______	______	______________
Total Weekly Cash Flow	______	______	______	______________

☑ Weekly Review & Milestones

Day	Top 1 Money Win	Slip/Challenge	Next Step / Fix
Monday	________________	________________	________________
Tuesday	________________	________________	________________
Wednesday	________________	________________	________________
Thursday	________________	________________	________________
Friday	________________	________________	________________
Saturday	________________	________________	________________
Sunday	________________	________________	________________

How to fill out the above table:

- **Top section** = the numbers (planned vs actual cash flow, just like a dashboard).
- **Bottom section** = reflection (daily wins + fixes), which keeps motivation alive.

🧠 Why You Must Include Savings While Killing Debt

This might sound strange—why save when you're paying off debt?

Because emergencies **will** happen.

If every extra dollar goes to debt with zero buffer, then one flat tire = back to the credit card.

We call it the **$500 Freedom Fund**.
Build it slowly. Even $10/week. Keep it separate. Use it *only* when needed.

> 💡 *"Savings buys you peace. Debt freedom buys you power. You deserve both."*

☑ 11.2– Monthly Reflection = Your Accountability Partner

"What gets reviewed, gets results."

At the end of each month, ask:

- What went well?
- What caught me off guard?
- What did I pay down?
- What did I overspend?

This is not to shame you—it's to strengthen your next move.

Use your numbers like feedback, not judgment.

📋 End-of-Month Reflection Worksheet

Month: ____

Reflection Prompt	Your Notes
☑ What went well?	____________________________
⚠ What caught me off guard?	____________________________
💳 What did I pay down?	____________________________
💸 What did I overspend on?	____________________________

🔧 Your Monthly Action Plan [example]

Use this structure weekly or monthly to track and adjust:

Section	Example
Income	$3,200
Expenses	$2,400
Debt Payment	$400
Savings Added	$100
Rollover to Next	$300
Notes	“Cutting out on dining-out, worked OUT”

This worksheet becomes your battle journal. Print it. Save it. Update it.

🧠 Case Study: Targeting Interest Wisely

✦Lisa's Financial Snapshot

Income & Expenses

Item	Monthly Amount
Net Income	**$3,200**
Fixed Expenses (rent $1,200, utilities $250, insurance $200, transport $250)	**$1,900**
Variable Expenses (groceries $400, phone $100, misc $150)	**$650**
Total Living Expenses	**$2,550**
Cash Flow Available for Debt	**$650**

Debt List

Debt	Balance	APR	APY (Effective)	Daily Interest Formula	Approx. Daily Interest
Credit Card	$6,000	27.99%	31.97%	6,000 × (0.2799 ÷ 365)	**$4.60/day ≈ $138/month**
Personal Loan	$9,500	8.5%	8.85%	9,500 × (0.085 ÷ 365)	**$2.22/day ≈ $68/month**

💡 Original Payment Habit

Lisa was splitting her **$650/mo debt budget** equally:

- **$325 → Credit Card**
- **$325 → Loan**

👉 This kept her feeling "fair" but was mathematically painful: the card's higher APR meant she was losing money faster than she was reducing principal.

🔄 Realization: Tracking Daily Interest

When Lisa started logging interest:

- The **credit card alone was adding $138/month** in new charges.
- The **loan only added $68/month**.
  She realized her "equal payments" were actually favoring the cheaper loan instead of attacking the most expensive debt.

🚀 Restructured Strategy (Avalanche Style)

- She switched to paying **only the loan minimum** ($150/mo).
- All remaining cash flow (**$500/mo**) went to the credit card.
- **Result:**
  - Credit Card wiped out in **4 months**.
  - Then she redirected the **full $650/mo** to the loan.

📊 Timeline

Phase	Focus Debt	Monthly Payment	Months	Interest Paid
1	Credit Card ($6,000)	$500 (min +extra)	4	≈ $400
2	Personal Loan ($9,500)	$650	~15	≈ $1,000
Total	**$15,500 → $0**	—	**19 months**	**≈ $1,400**

✅ **Key Lesson:** Lisa stopped "splitting payments" and instead killed the **most expensive money first**. Avalanche shaved off thousands in potential interest and freed her in less than 2 years.

> 💡 *Strategy: Kill the most expensive money first—even if it's not the biggest balance "Avalanche Style"*

🔍 Daily Interest vs. Amortized Interest Explained

Credit cards and lines of credit charge **daily interest**—your balance grows every single day it sits unpaid.

Loans and mortgages often use **amortized interest**—the structure hides how much is going to interest at the start.

That's why early loan payments barely touch the principal.

Daily interest drains you quietly. Amortized interest drains you slowly. But both can be hacked with discipline.

📋 Daily Interest vs. Amortized Interest – Real example

Feature	Credit Card (Daily Interest)	Student Loan (Amortized Interest)
Balance Example	$2,800	$9,000
APR	25.99%	6.5%
How Interest is Calculated	Charged **daily** on the unpaid balance: $2,800 × (0.2599 ÷ 365) ≈ **$1.99/day**	Built into fixed monthly payments; interest is front-loaded in early months
Monthly Interest Cost	~$60 (if no payment is made)	~$49 (first month of a 10-year term)
What Happens if You Only Pay Minimum	Balance shrinks very slowly; interest keeps compounding daily	Payment stays the same, but most of it goes to interest at the beginning
Effect on Principal	Very little reduction unless you pay more than the minimum	Principal reduction accelerates only in later years
Psychological Trap	"It's just a couple dollars a day" → adds up silently	"I'm paying every month" → but early payments barely touch the balance
Best Hack	Pay down aggressively or transfer to 0% APR	Add extra to principal each month to cut years off the loan

"Credit cards bleed you daily, loans bleed you slowly"

🛠 When to Use a Line of Credit (Without Wrecking Yourself)

Used poorly, a line of credit is a trap.
Used wisely, it's a tool.

Franck used a $3,000 personal line of credit at 11.5% to pay off a credit card at 28.5%.

He transferred the balance from the Credit Card to the LOC, saving $510/year in interest.

But here's what he **did right**:

- He had a payment plan to pay it off in 6 months.
- He *stopped* using the old credit card.
- He set up **auto-pay** to never miss a due date.

That's how a line of credit becomes a sword—not a chain.

📋 When to Use a Line of Credit (LOC) Wisely

Scenario	Bad Use (Trap)	Smart Use (Franck's Example)
Starting Debt	Keeps balance on high-interest credit card (28.5%)	Transfers $3,000 balance to LOC at 11.5%
Interest Cost	~$855/year (28.5% of $3,000)	~$345/year (11.5% of $3,000) → **$510 saved/ year**
Plan	No structured payoff plan; pays minimums only	Clear 6-month payoff plan with fixed monthly payments
Old Credit Card	Keeps using it, racks up more debt	Stops using it entirely
Payments	Often manual and inconsistent; risk of missed payments	Auto-pay set up to cover LOC each month
Outcome	Debt snowballs, interest grows faster	Debt reduced faster, less interest paid
Metaphor	A chain that traps you	A sword that cuts debt

☑ **The LOC itself isn't good or bad** — it depends on the behavior and plan.

🔄 Rewire Your Story

"I've never stuck with a plan. Every time I try, I fall behind."

You say:

> *"This plan is mine. I'm not guessing anymore—I'm choosing. And when I choose, I win."*

We often give up because we're copying someone else's system.
This time, you're building one that matches your life, your habits, your rhythm.

That's why it will work.

💬 Written just for you

> *"Discipline isn't punishment. It's freedom on the other side of discomfort."*

📌 Chapter Summary: What You've Conquered

Progress doesn't come from perfection. It comes from a plan that feels like home.

- **Weekly cash flow = daily control.** Stop waiting for the month to end.

- **Emergency savings matter—even while paying debt.** Don't break your stride for a crisis.
- **Interest is the real enemy.** Know your daily charges and target them with power.
- **A line of credit is a tool, not a toy.** Plan its use or lose its benefit.
- **Reflection isn't guilt—it's guidance.** Look back to adjust your path forward.

✵ Next Step

In Chapter 12, we take a hard look at **emergencies, sabotage, and how to stay calm when life throws chaos your way.** Because let's face it—life will happen. But this time, you'll be ready.

This page is left intentionally blank

CHAPTER 12

A Sample Walkthrough

One Family's Path from Buried to Free

> *"Sometimes we need to see it to believe it. This chapter is that proof."*

☑ 12.1– From Stuck to Strategic: Meet Carla and David

Carla and David were a regular couple living in Florida. Both worked full-time. They weren't broke, but they were **tired**—tired of juggling bills, tired of seeing their credit card balances go nowhere, tired of talking about debt but never making real progress.

🔧 Their Monthly Game Plan Looked Like This:

- Total Income: $6,200/month
- Fixed Expenses: $3,700 (including rent, utilities, gas, food, insurance)
- Emergency savings: $100/month

- Debt payment: $678.05
- Cash Flow: $ 1,721.95

Here is how we found the "Cash Flow" of $1,721.95

Step 1 — Start with total income
$6,200.00

Step 2 — Subtract fixed expenses
$6,200 - $3,700 = $2,500.00

Step 3 — Subtract emergency savings
$2,500 - $100 = $2,400.00

Step 4 — Subtract debt payments
$2,400 - $678.05 = **$1,721.95**

☑ Your **cash flow is $1,721.95**

You have **$1,721.95** left after covering expenses, savings, and debt payments.

> *"We used to feel like we couldn't breathe. But after one month of doing this, we could see the light."*
>
> *✦Carla*

Their total debt was $33,000:

- Credit Cards: $9,000 @ 26.99%
- Auto Loan: $12,000 @ 8.5%
- Personal Loan: $7,000 @ 10.9%
- Store Card: $5,000 @ 28.99%

Minimum total monthly payments: **$678.05 (column 2 below)**

Debt	Min Payment	APR	Months to Pay Off	Interest Paid
Credit Card A	$180.00	26.99	20 years +	Over 10k
Auto Loan	$246.20	8.5	60	$2,771.90
Personal Loan	$151.85	10.9	60	$2,110.89
Store Card	$100.00	28.99	20 years +	Over 10k
Total	**$678.05**			

According to their lenders' schedules, they would be in debt for **5 years minimum on the loans and over 20 years on the credit cards,** and pay **thousands in interest**.

They didn't know where to start.
Until they sat down, took inventory, and said:

"This ends now. We're tired—but we're not powerless."

🔍 12.2– The First Step: Mapping the Terrain

They did what this book is teaching you to do:

1. List all debts: balance, interest rate, minimum payment

Debt	Min Payment	APR
Credit Card A	$180.00	26.99
Auto Loan	$246.20	8.5
Personal Loan	$151.85	10.9
Store Card	$100.00	28.99

2. Sort them by **interest rate** (They chose the Avalanche Method)

Debt	Min Payment	APR
Store Card	$100.00	28.99
Credit Card A	$180.00	26.99
Personal Loan	$151.85	10.9
Auto Loan	$246.20	8.5

Build a spreadsheet to track payments

3. Use **cash flow** to budget extra toward highest-interest debt

Debt 1: Store Card

Using the avalanche method and applying your **entire $1,721.95 cash flow** to the **Store Card ($5,000 @ 28.99%)** on top of its minimum payment ($100):

Results

- **Months to Pay Off:** 3 months
- **Total Interest Paid:** $238.09

Payoff Table (first and last months)

Month	Payment	Interest	Principal	Remaining Balance
1	$1,821.95	$120.79	$1,701.16	$3,298.84
2	$1,821.95	$79.69	$1,742.26	$1,556.59
3	$1,594.19	$37.60	$1,556.59	$0.00

After debt 1, you could redirect the freed-up $1,821.95 + the next debt's minimum payment to your next highest APR account to keep the avalanche rolling.

Amount freed-up: $1,721.95 cash flow + $100 used to be the minimum payment on Store card

Minimum payment on Debt #2 (Credit Card A): $ 180

Debt 2: Credit Card A

Once the Store Card is paid off, the payment going to **Credit Card A** should be:

$1,721.95 (cash flow) + $100 (freed Store Card min) + $180 (CC A min) = **$2,001.95/month.**

Quick note – Keep in mind – But don't stress about it – valid for every debt you pay "minimum-only": Assuming you spent the first **3 months** killing the Store Card while still paying **$180** minimum due on Credit Card A at **26.99% APR**; the monthly interest on $9,000 is about **$202.42**, which is **more than $180**, so the balance creeps up slightly, because you keep paying only the minimum. Don't stress, it's only temporary. *For the sake of simplicity, we will keep minimums locked (see section above 12.2 table 1).*

Let's tackle Credit Card A ($2,001.95/mo)

Month	Payment	Interest	Principal	Remaining
1	2,001.95	203.97	1,797.98	7,270.82
2	2,001.95	163.53	1,838.42	5,432.40
3	2,001.95	122.18	1,879.77	3,552.64

4	2,001.95	79.90	1,922.05	1,630.59
5	1,667.27	36.67	1,630.59	0.00

Interest: $606.25

Total (all 8 months):

- **Months:** 8 (3 months min-only + 5 avalanche)

Debt #3: Personal Loan

For **Personal Loan ($7,000 @ 10.9%)** using the avalanche method:

- **Minimum Payment:** $151.85 (based on 5-year amortization)
- **Avalanche Payment** After Store Card and Credit Card A Paid Off: $2,153.80/month
- **Months to Pay Off:** 4 months
- **Total Interest Paid:** $139.73

Payoff Table

Month	Payment	Interest	Principal	Remaining Balance
1	2,153.80	$63.58	$2,090.21	$4,909.79
2	2,153.80	$44.60	$2,109.20	$2,800.58
3	2,153.80	$25.44	$2,128.36	$672.22
4	$678.33	$6.11	$672.22	$0.00

After this, your entire **$2,153.80** ($2153.80 + minimum payment on personal loan paid off $151.85) payment can be rolled into the final debt — the auto loan

Debt #4: Auto Loan

For Auto Loan ($12,000 @ 8.5%) in the avalanche plan:

- Minimum Payment: $246.20 (5-year amortization)
- Avalanche Payment After Store Card, Credit Card A and Personal Loan Paid Off: $2,400.00/month
- Months to Pay Off: 6 months
- Total Interest Paid: $261.70

Payoff Table

Month	Payment	Interest	Principal	Remaining Balance
1	$2,400.00	$85.00	$2,315.00	$9,685.00
2	$2,400.00	$68.60	$2,331.39	$7,353.61
3	$2,400.00	$52.09	$2,347.91	$5,005.70
4	$2,400.00	$35.46	$2,364.54	$2,641.16
5	$2,400.00	$18.71	$2,381.29	$259.87
6	$261.71	$1.84	$259.87	$0.00

Payoff Summary

Debt	Months to $0	Total Interest Paid
Store Card ($5,000 @ 28.99%)	3	$238.09
Credit Card A ($9,000 @ 26.99%)	8*	$1,215.07
Personal Loan ($7,000 @ 10.9%)	4	$139.73

Debt	Months to $0	Total Interest Paid
Auto Loan ($12,000 @ 8.5%)	6	$261.70
TOTAL	**21 months**	**$1,854.59**

**Includes 3 months of minimum-only payments while the store card was being cleared, plus 5 avalanche months.*

Carla and David finally realized they could tackle these debts in 21 months vs 5 to 20+ years that the lenders had predicted! All they needed was to write down everything, have a plan, follow the plan with strict discipline.

12.3- Debt Elimination in action – Step by step process

Here are the basic "rules of game 1":

- Payday in examples are MONTHLY. You can adapt and use weekly or bi-weekly numbers.
- We are using the AVALANCHE method
- We are using a 0% interest Credit Card as the TOOL
- Your checking account number is #12345

Pre-requisite #1 of Game 1: you need an extra checking account, besides the one that is receiving your paycheck. Shop around and choose a checking account that has no monthly fee (or very low monthly fee) and no minimum balance restriction. The less it costs you to keep this account in good standing, the better.

For the sake of this example, let's give your second checking account a number #67890

Pre-requisite #2 of Game 1: Apply for a 0% interest credit card. Once this card is received, you will transfer your debts onto this card ! I the current example, we are choosing the "Avalanche method", which means you will transfer first the highestAPR debt onto the 0% interest credit card.

If the limit of the 0% interest credit card is not enough to cover all your card debts, we will go step by step: Transfer as much as you can. Keep making minimum payments on the rest, until your credit limit on the 0% interest credit card is available to cover your other debts.

Let's use these numbers as illustration for Game 1:

Debt Account	**Starting Balance**	**APR %**	**Minimum Payment**	**Type**
Store Card	$4000	29.99	120	revolving
Personal Loan	$6000	18	180	installment
Auto Loan	$9000	8	250	installment
Student Loan	$2500	5.5	100	Installment
Total	**$21,500**		**$650**	

The store card will be in the above example the first amount to transfer to the 0% interest credit card.

Note: Transferring a debt from one card to another does cost 3% to 5%, but with the debt elimination strategy we are applying, it does not hurt your plan.

Here is the walkthrough on how to dispatch your paycheck:

Section 1: Let's write down the basics

Step 1: On payday, your salary is sent directly to your checking account#12345 or is given to you in the form of a check. (e.g., $3,500). You deposit the check into account #12345

Monthly Income (Net)
3500

Step 1.1: What is your list of expenses?

- what is the total of expenses you can pay with a credit card ? (e.g., $800).
- what is the total of expenses must be paid in CASH or Bank Transfer? (e.g., $2,000).

Summary

Column 1	Column 2	Column 3
Total Monthly Expenses	**Cash-only Expenses**	**Credit-eligible Expenses**
2800	2000	800

Detail Column 2

Expense (Cash-Only)	Monthly Amount
Rent	1200
Utilities (cash/ACH only)	150

Store Card or Credit Card- Minimum Payment (cash/ACH)	120
Personal Loan - Minimum Payment (cash/ACH)	180
Auto Loan - Minimum Payment (ACH)	250
Student Loan - Minimum Payment (ACH)	100
Total CASH-ONLY Expense	**2,000**

Detail Column 3

Expense (Tool-Eligible)	**Monthly Amount**
Groceries	400
Gas/Transport	180
Insurance (allows card)	120
Phone	60
Subscriptions	40
Total expenses that can be paid with a CARD	**800**

Step 1.2: What is your Cash Flow?

Formula to know your cash flow:

All income - All expenses = Cash Flow (e.g., $700).

Monthly Income (Net)	**Total Monthly Expenses**	***Cash-only Expenses***	***Credit-eligible Expenses***	**Monthly Free Cash Flow**
3500	2800	*2000*	*800*	700

Section 2: Choose a Tool

For example, we will choose a 0% interest credit card (see above **rules of game 1**)

Here is how we will be using this tool:

Step 2.1: After dropping your paycheck into checking account # 12345

Transfer the total amount of CASH ONLY expenses into checking account # 67890. (e.g., $2,000).

Tip: Transfers from one account to the other inside the same bank are usually FREE of charge. If your accounts are not in the same bank and you will have a fee, just for transferring this amount, just write yourself a check from account #12345 and deposit into account #67890, that will be a FREE transaction.

After this transaction, here is how your accounts will look:

Transaction	Account#67890	Account#12345
Income Received	Transfer from #12345	What is left after transfer
3,500	2,000	1,500

Step 2.2: Let's pay <u>wisely</u>

Pay CASH-ONLY bills out of account #67890 only

CASH-ONLY bills mean all ***cashonly*** *bills + all debt* ***minimums*** *that don't accept card payment.*

(See Detail column 2 above)

You can either pay all these bills on the same date, or pay them each close to their due date (2 to 3 days before). Be very mindful of the impact payments have on your credit score health.

Expense (Cash-Only)	Monthly Amount
Rent	1200
Utilities (cash/ACH only)	150
Store Card - Minimum Payment (cash/ACH)	120
Personal Loan - Minimum Payment (cash/ACH)	180
Auto Loan - Minimum Payment (ACH)	250
Student Loan - Minimum Payment (ACH)	100
	2000

Step 2.3: Strategic payment

2.3.1: After putting aside, the amount exclusively reserved for Cash-only expenses, the amount left on the initial checking account #12345 will now be deposited into our debt elimination tool, our 0% interest credit card **"The Tool"**.

Using our example, $800 will be applied as payment on the 0% interest credit card to pay for the debts that can be paid with a credit card.

Expense (Tool-Eligible)	Monthly Amount
Groceries	400
Gas/Transport	180
Insurance (allows card)	120
Phone	60
Subscriptions	40
	800

Use the 0% interest Credit Card **"The Tool"** to pay every expense you listed as crediteligible (groceries, gas, etc... see above detail **Column 3**).

2.3.2: The checking account #12345 now will only have the cash-flow as balance (e.g., $700)

Remember in the example - Step 1.2 above (Cash Flow), when your income comes IN and your total expenses goes OUT, the "extra" left is the "cash flow".

- Scenario 1: The "Old way" of doing things, this cash flow amount would eventually appear in your checking account, and could be perceived as "extra" money. You might then have a tendency to use it on useless item purchases or put it on a low-interest savings account; now you know better!
- Scenario 2: Using our current strategy this "extra" **cash flow** (e.g., $700) automatically becomes an **extra payment**, that will get you debt-free faster.
    - Option 1 in scenario 2– Pre-requisite 2 above – We have chosen the Avalanche method to pay-off our debt. If the total amount of the highest interest card was the one transferred to the 0% interest credit card that we are using as "Tool", then, the cash flow left on the account can be deposited into the 0% interest credit card directly (our tool).
    - Option 2 in scenario 2– Pre-requisite 2 above – We have chosen the Avalanche method

to pay-off our debt. If the highest interest card amount was not transferred to the 0% interest credit card, then you will write a check from the checking account #12345 and make an extra payment to the highest interest credit card (Avalanche method)

Notes & tips:

- If your card/tool doesn't allow paying certain debts directly, send the **extra** to checking and pay the lender via ACH or check the same day.
- If your issuer doesn't allow overpayments (credit balances), transfer **only** the amount you plan to spend on cardeligible expenses **plus** the extra you'll immediately push to the target debt.
- For HELOC/PLOC versions, the same worksheet structure applies—swap the **tool APR**, and (optionally) model a "chunk" transfer to a target loan, then deposit income directly to the HELOC/PLOC to reduce average daily balance.

🧠 Lynn's Case Study Breakdown: The Avalanche in Action

What do we KNOW:

- **Monthly Net Income:** $4,500

Expenses:

- Total Fixed Expenses: $1,800 *(rent, utilities, insurance, subscriptions)*
- Total Variable Expenses: $600 *(groceries, gas, entertainment)*
- **Total: $1800+$600 = $2400**
- **Expense breakdown (same as above** – separated by type of payment accepted)
- Cash-Only Expenses: $2,000 *(from fixed + variable that can't be paid with a card/PLOC)*
- Credit-Eligible Expenses: $400 *(from fixed + variable that can be paid with the tool)*

Total: $2000+$400 = $2400

- **Total Debt Owed:** $22,000 across 4 accounts
    1. Store Card – $5,000 @ **28.99%** APR
    2. Credit Card – $3,500 @ **26.99%** APR
    3. Personal Loan – $8,000 @ **12.99%** APR
    4. Auto Loan – $5,500 @ **7.99%** APR
- **Monthly Debt Minimums (all accounts):**

Debt Account	Scaled Minimum Payment
Store Card	$225
Credit Card	$160
Personal Loan	$420
Auto Loan	$320

Total: $1,125 ☑

- **Emergency Fund savings**: $500
- **Monthly Cash Flow (after all expenses): $475** available to add to debt payments

Here is the "old way of doing things" and the "old result" we do NOT want

If you only pay the fixed minimums listed above:

Debt Account	Months to Pay Off	Interest Paid
Store Card	33 months	$2,255.47
Credit Card	31 months	$1,372.45
Personal Loan	22 months	$1,008.13
Auto Loan	19 months	$360.64

Summary:

- Longest debt payoff time: 33 months (Store Card)
- Total interest paid across all debts: $4,996.68

This means, without this book's guidance, it would take you about **2 years and 9 months to be completely debt-free, paying nearly $5,000 in interest**

Let's work together on our new strategy!

Strategy Chosen: Avalanche Method –

We keep the same numbers:

Step 1: Focus all extra payments on the highest APR debt: Store Card 28.99% APR, while paying minimums on the others.

💳 **Store Card Payoff** – Avalanche Method (with Hidden Interest Shown)

(Interest calculated as Balance × APR ÷ 12)

Month	Payment	Interest	Principal	Ending Balance
1	700.00	120.79	579.21	4,420.79
2	700.00	106.80	593.20	3,827.59
3	700.00	92.47	607.53	3,220.06
4	700.00	77.79	622.21	2,597.85
5	700.00	62.76	637.24	1,960.61
6	700.00	47.37	652.63	1,307.97
7	700.00	31.60	668.40	639.57
8	655.02	15.45	639.57	0.00

> **How to read column 2:** *Payment*
>
> *$225 is the "minimum amount due" on store card, every month. Plus, the cash flow of $475 (the money left after all bills are paid). $225 + $475 = $700*
>
> *cash flow we have left every month after paying all the bills, the "extra".*

Summary:

- **Months to $0:** 8
- **Total interest paid:** $555.02

Key Takeaways:

- That **$225 "minimum"** isn't all going to principal — a big chunk each month is **interest disguised in the payment.**

- At the start, **over 17% of the $700** goes to interest; by the final month, it's almost **all principal**.
- If you had paid only the $225 minimum, the store card would take **years** to clear and cost **thousands in extra interest**.

Next up:

Step 2: 💳 Credit Card Payoff @ 26.99%

Facts we are working with here:

- The Store Card is now **paid off**, so its former **minimum payment $225 + $475 extra** are now applied to the Credit Card we are paying now in Step 2.
- All other debts (Personal Loan, Auto Loan) continue getting their minimum payments only.
- APR for the Credit Card is **26.99%**.
- Monthly payment toward this card now = **its old minimum $160 + $475 extra + Store Card minimum $225 = $860**

Credit Card ($3,500 @ 26.99%) using avalanche after Debt #1 is cleared:

Payment applied: $860/month (Credit Card's $160 minimum + $700 freed from Store Card payoff)

Month	Payment	Interest	Principal	Ending Balance
1	860.00	78.72	781.28	2,718.72
2	860.00	61.15	798.85	1,919.87

Month	Payment	Interest	Principal	Ending Balance
3	860.00	43.18	816.82	1,103.05
4	860.00	24.81	835.19	267.86
5	273.88	6.02	267.86	0.00

Summary

- **Months to $0:** 5
- **Total interest paid:** $213.88

What's happening here

- In the first month, **over $78** of your payment is **just interest** — meaning only $781 actually reduces the balance.
- By the last month, almost **100% of your payment** goes to principal.
- Paying only the **$160 minimum** would stretch this debt into **years** and cost **thousands** more in interest.

Next up:

Step 3: 💵 Personal Loan Payoff – Avalanche Method (with Hidden Interest)

Starting Point:

- **Balance:** $8,000
- **APR:** 12.99%
- **Minimum Payment:** $420

- **Extra Payment from Avalanche:** $860 (Credit Card min $160 paid off + $700 extra from Store Card paid off)
- **Total Monthly Payment to Personal Loan:** $420 + $860 = $1,280

Personal Loan ($8,000 @ 12.99%) using avalanche after Debt #1 & 2 are cleared:

Payment applied: $1,280/month (Personal Loan's $420 minimum + $700 freed from Store Card payoff + $160 freed from Credit Card payoff)

Month	Payment	Interest	Principal	Ending Balance
1	1,280.00	86.60	1,193.40	6,806.60
2	1,280.00	73.68	1,206.32	5,600.28
3	1,280.00	60.62	1,219.38	4,380.90
4	1,280.00	47.42	1,232.58	3,148.33
5	1,280.00	34.08	1,245.92	1,902.41
6	1,280.00	20.59	1,259.41	643.00
7	649.96	6.96	643.00	0.00

Summary

- **Months to $0:** 7
- **Total interest paid:** $329.96

What's happening here

- In the first month, **$86.67** of your payment is **just interest**, but because the APR is much lower than the Store or Credit Card, most of your payment goes to principal from the start.

- The loan is paid off in **7 months** after starting Avalanche payments on it.
- That $1,280/month will now roll to your **last debt (Auto Loan)** if you continue the Avalanche.

Next up

Step 4 – Knocking down our last debt, the auto loan

Now that the **Personal Loan** is paid off, the **$1,280/month** you were sending to it (its $420 minimum + $860 extra from the previous debts) rolls down to the **Auto Loan**

🚙 Auto Loan Payoff – Avalanche Method (with Hidden Interest)

Starting Point:

- **Balance:** $5,500
- **APR:** 7.99%
- **Minimum Payment (locked):** $320
- **Extra Payment from Avalanche:** $1,280 (Personal Loan min $420 + $860 extra)
- **Total Monthly Payment to Auto Loan:** $1,600

Auto Loan ($5,500 @ 7.99%) using avalanche after Debt #1, 2 & 3 are cleared:

Payment applied: $1,600/month (Auto Loan's $320 minimum + $700 freed from Store Card payoff + $160 freed from Credit Card payoff + $420 freed from Personal Loan payoff)

Month	Payment	Interest	Principal	Ending Balance
1	1,600.00	36.62	1,563.38	3,936.62
2	1,600.00	26.21	1,573.79	2,362.83
3	1,600.00	15.73	1,584.27	778.56
4	783.75	5.18	778.56	0.00

Summary

- **Months to $0:** 4
- **Total interest paid:** $83.75

Key Notes for Readers

- Because the APR is low, the interest cost each month is minimal compared to earlier debts. The Auto Loan disappears **in less than 4 months** once it becomes the Avalanche target.
- Total interest over the Auto Loan payoff period = **only about $84**, compared to **thousands** in interest avoided on high-APR debts earlier in the process.

💬 What They Said After

> *"We used to think debt payoff was about 'being good with money.' But it's about being consistent with a plan. It became a rhythm. Like going to the gym. We got addicted to seeing the numbers drop."*

🔄 Rewire Your Story

"This plan works for others but not for me."

That voice is fear. It's your past speaking louder than your progress.

Say this instead:

> *"I have never had a plan this clear. I am capable of following it. I am not stuck—I am starting."*

We often believe others are just "better with money."
But the truth is: they had support, clarity, and time.
Now, so do you.

Every step you take in this book is proof that this time, your story ends differently.

💬 Written just for you

> *"Success isn't about intensity—it's about consistency. $200/month of strategy beats $2,000 of guessing."*

📌 Chapter Summary: What You've Conquered

> *Freedom is not a mystery. It's math—with courage.*

- **Big numbers don't need big income.** They need smart strategies and consistent effort.
- **Your debt doesn't need 5 years.** With a plan, you can cut that time by more than half.

- **Interest is your silent enemy.** Target the highest ones first to stop the bleeding.
- **Visualizing your path keeps you on it.** Monthly tracking = daily motivation.
- **You can do this.** It's already been done—with less income, more chaos, and fewer tools.

✸ Next Step

In Chapter 13, we'll tackle what happens *when life doesn't go as planned*. Spoiler: it's not the end. It's just a reroute.

This page is left intentionally blank

CHAPTER 13

Your Turn

Build Your Strategy (Your Personal Playbook)

> *"It's no longer about learning. It's about doing. This chapter is yours."*

☑ 13.1– From Observer to Architect: You're Now in Control

Let's pause for a moment.

Think back to where you were when you started this book.

Maybe you felt ashamed, overwhelmed, or completely out of options.

Maybe the numbers looked impossible. Maybe you thought, *"I'm not good at this."*

And yet... here you are.

With clarity. With tools. With knowledge.

And most importantly—with the power to make a plan that fits **your real life.**

This chapter is not theoretical. It's practical.

It's where you move from **watching the game** to **calling the plays.**

Because financial freedom doesn't start with perfection. It starts with **a plan you're willing to commit to for 30 days at a time.**

Let's build that now.

🔍 13.2– Key Concepts, Simply Explained

📃 Rollover Strategy

Every time you finish paying off one debt, you take that **minimum payment amount** and roll it over into the next one.
This builds **momentum** and shortens your total payoff timeline dramatically.

Think of it like a snowball rolling downhill—picking up power and speed.

🔁 Recalculating Every 3 Months

Life shifts. Income changes. Emergencies happen.
This is why you'll revisit your plan every 90 days.
That way, it stays realistic, relevant, and adjustable.

🧠 Tracking = Truth

Don't rely on memory. Use the worksheets in this book to stay accountable.

Tracking is not about guilt. It's about **proof that you're doing the work.**

🔧 13.3– The Mini Framework: Build Your Personal Debt Strategy

Here's what you'll fill out (with examples inserted):

Step 1: List All Debts

Debt Name	Balance	Interest Rate	Minimum Payment	Monthly Goal	Strategy
Chase Card	$2,600	22.99%	$80	$200	Avalanche
Auto Loan	$7,400	8.5%	$260	$260	Minimum
Store Card	$1,800	28.99%	$50	$300	Snowball

Step 2: Weekly Cash Flow Check-In

Week	Income In	Expenses Out	Rollover to Debt	Notes
Week 1	$1,200	$940	$160	On track
Week 2	$1,200	$1,020	$80	Groceries went over
Week 3	$1,200	$950	$150	Cut streaming service
Week 4	$1,200	$900	$200	Best week!

Step 3: 3-Month Progress Tracker

Month	Total Paid Toward Debt	Total Interest Paid	Debts Closed	Wins
Month 1	$850	$150	0	Made 4 extra payments
Month 2	$1,100	$110	1	Store card closed!
Month 3	$1,200	$80	1	Emergency savings at $300

"When the numbers show progress, your brain stops doubting your effort."

🔗 Final Tool: "Your First 90 Days Debt-Free" Worksheet

Week	Focus / Action Step	Planned Payment or Saving	Actual	Reflection / Win
1	Cancel unused subscriptions	$______	$______	____________________
2	Create zero-based budget	$______	$______	____________________
3	Pay extra on [Debt Name]	$______	$______	____________________
4	Cut dining out by 50%	$______	$______	____________________
5	Sell 1–2 unused items	$______	$______	____________________
6	Check credit report	$______	$______	____________________
7	Pay extra on [Debt Name]	$______	$______	____________________
8	Meal plan to cut groceries	$______	$______	____________________

Week	Focus / Action Step	Planned Payment or Saving	Actual	Reflection / Win
9	Add $50 to emergency fund	$______	$______	________________
10	No-spend weekend	$______	$______	________________
11	Pay extra on [Debt Name]	$______	$______	________________
12	Review progress & celebrate	$______	$______	________________

- **Week column** keeps the timeline visible.
- **Focus / Action Step** gives one practical task.
- **Planned vs. Actual** shows money goals.
- **Reflection / Win** builds momentum and accountability.

🧠 Case Study: Nicole's Debt Snowball Turnaround in 23 Months

✦Nicole is a **37-year-old nursing assistant** and single mother of two. She earns **$3,900/month after taxes** and rents a modest 2-bedroom apartment. For years, her credit card balances and a personal loan have been a source of constant stress.

Determined to take back control, Nicole adopted the **Snowball Method** — focusing on paying off her smallest balance first while making minimum payments on all other debts. This gave her quick wins and the motivation to keep going.

Her monthly expenses are:

Category	Amount
Rent & Utilities	$1,600
Groceries	$650
Transportation	$300
Insurance	$200
Childcare/School	$250
Phone & Internet	$150
Misc. Living Costs	$300
Total Expenses	**$3,450**

This leaves $450/month cash flow available for debt repayment — plus any minimum payments already budgeted.

Debts (Before applying her strategy)

Debt Account	Balance	APR	Minimum Payment
Credit Card #1	$1,200	22.9%	$60
Credit Card #2	$3,000	19.5%	$90
Personal Loan	$6,500	9.5%	$210

Nicole's Strategy:

- Wants to use the **Snowball Method**
- Tracks spending in a notebook each week
- Recalculates goals every 3 months
- Keeps a $150 emergency cushion

Why Snowball Method?

Nicole chose **Snowball** because:

- She wanted **quick wins** to keep her motivated.
- Seeing a card get paid off completely helps her **stick to the plan**.
- Mathematically, Avalanche saves more on interest, but Snowball gave her the emotional momentum she needed.

How Nicole's Snowball Plan will work:

1. **List debts from smallest to largest balance** (ignore APR at this step).
2. **Pay all minimums** on every debt.
3. Apply **all extra money** to the smallest balance first.
4. Once a debt is paid off, **roll its payment** into the next smallest.

Order:

Order	Debt Account	Balance	APR	Minimum Payment
1	Credit Card #1	$1,200	22.9%	$60
2	Credit Card #2	$3,000	19.5%	$90
3	Personal Loan	$6,500	9.5%	$210

Debt 1: Credit Card #1 ($1,200 @ 22.9%) in the Snowball Method:

Month	**Payment**	**Interest**	**Principal**	**Ending Balance**
1	$510	$22.90	$487.10	$712.90
2	$510	$13.62	$496.38	$216.52

Month	Payment	Interest	Principal	Ending Balance
3	$220.48	$4.13	$216.35	$0.00

Notes: Monthly payment: *$60 minimum + $450 cash flow = $510 (until final month when balance is smaller).* **Payoff time:** *3 months*

Debt 2: Credit Card #2 ($3,000 @ 19.5%) using the Snowball Method after Phase 1 payoff:

Payment applied: $600/month ($510 snowball from Cash Flow + Credit Card #1 paid off + $90 Credit Card 2 minimum)

Month	Payment	Interest	Principal	Ending Balance
1	600.00	48.75	551.25	2,448.75
2	600.00	39.79	560.21	1,888.54
3	600.00	30.69	569.31	1,319.23
4	600.00	21.44	578.56	740.67
5	600.00	12.04	587.96	152.70
6	155.19	2.48	152.70	0.00

Summary: Months to $0: *6* - **Total interest paid:** *$155.19*

Debt 3: Personal Loan ($6,500 @ 9.5%) in the Snowball Method after Phase 2 payoff:

Payment applied: $810/month ($600 snowball from Cash Flow + Credit Card #1 & 2 paid Off + $210 personal loan minimum)

Month	Payment	Interest	Principal	Ending Balance
1	810.00	51.46	758.54	5,741.46
2	810.00	45.45	764.55	4,976.91
3	810.00	39.40	770.60	4,206.31
4	810.00	33.30	776.70	3,429.61
5	810.00	27.15	782.85	2,646.76
6	810.00	20.95	789.05	1,857.72

Month	Payment	Interest	Principal	Ending Balance
7	810.00	14.71	795.29	1,062.42
8	810.00	8.41	801.59	260.83
9	262.90	2.06	260.83	0.00

Summary: Months to $0: *9* - **Total interest paid:** *$242.90*

Debt 4: Auto Loan ($5,500 @ 7.99%) in the Snowball Method after Phase 3 payoff:

Payment applied: $1,130/month ($810 snowball from Cash Flow+ Credit Card 1 & 2 paid off + Personal Loan paid off + $320 auto loan minimum)

Month	Payment	Interest	Principal	Ending Balance
1	1,130.00	36.62	1,093.38	4,406.62
2	1,130.00	29.34	1,100.66	3,305.96
3	1,130.00	22.01	1,107.99	2,197.97
4	1,130.00	14.63	1,115.37	1,082.61
5	1,089.82	7.21	1,082.61	0.00

Summary: Months to $0: *5* - **Total interest paid:** *$109.82*

Recap Summary of the Debt Elimination process using the Snowball Method

Phase	Debt	Balance	APR	Payment Applied	Months to $0	Interest Paid
1	Credit Card #1	$1,200	22.90%	$510	3	$64.63
2	Credit Card #2	$3,000	19.50%	$600	6	$155.19
3	Personal Loan	$6,500	9.50%	$810	9	$242.90
4	Auto Loan	$5,500	7.99%	$1,130	5	$109.82
TOTAL	—	**$16,200**	—	—	**23 months**	**$572.54**

Snowball Highlights:

- **Total Debt Paid:** $16,200 (not including interest)
- **Total Interest Paid:** $572.54
- **Time to Debt Freedom: 23 months**
- **Interest Savings vs. Original 5-Month Plan:** $54.28 saved on Credit Card #1
- **Momentum Growth:** Payment amount snowballs from **$510 → $600 → $810 → $1,130** as each debt is cleared.
- **Psychological Boost:** The quicker 3-month win on the first card gives Nicole an even stronger burst of motivation for tackling the next debts.

Nicole's Additional Strategies

- **Weekly Expense Tracking:** She records every expense in a notebook to stay accountable.
- **Quarterly Goal Review:** Every 3 months, she recalculates her debt payoff projections.
- **Small Rewards:** Each time she clears a debt, she celebrates with a low-cost family treat.
- **Emergency Cushion:** She maintains a buffer amount so unexpected expenses don't derail progress.

End Result:

Nicole will be **debt-free in under 2 years**, paying almost **$2,000 less in interest** than if she stuck to minimum payments. The speed of the first payoff gave her the momentum to see the plan through, proving that emotional wins can be just as powerful as mathematical ones.

She started by saying, *"This won't work for me."*
Now she says,

> *"This is MY plan. And I'm finally breathing."*

🗒 Self-Check: My Monthly Action Plan

Purpose: Build a one-page monthly strategy to follow.

Steps:

1. Write down all income for the month.
2. Subtract fixed expenses.
3. List flexible expenses and plan where you'll cut.
4. Determine total extra you can put toward debt.
5. Assign your target debt and minimums.
6. Set a small buffer/savings goal if needed.

Hands-on Example:

- Income: $4,200

- Fixed Expenses: $2,600
- Flexible Expenses: $900 → Cut $200 (eating out + gym)
- Debt Payments: $700 ($300 minimums + $400 extra to target)
- Savings Goal: $100

🔄 Rewire Your Story

"I always start strong, but I never finish..."

That story isn't your truth. It's your fear.
Your brain is trying to protect you from disappointment.
But that fear is outdated. You're not winging it this time.

Say this instead:

> *"This plan is built for me. I'm not perfect—but I'm prepared."*

Each worksheet, each check-in, each number on the page—is a **bridge** from where you are to where you want to be.

This is not about discipline alone. It's about **designing your success** ahead of time.

💬 Written just for you

> *"You don't need a new life. You just need a new pattern. And this is the pattern that sets you free."*

Now you have your plan. In the chapters ahead, we'll see how to protect it—and where to go next once the debt is gone.

📌 Chapter Summary: What You've Conquered

- A **clear debt list** with strategy assignments
- A **weekly income/expense tracker**
- A **monthly action sheet** that keeps you focused
- A **recalibration routine** every 3 months
- A **real plan** that reflects your real life

🌟 Next Step: It's Working. Keep Working It.

Chapter 14 is about building protection and staying ready—for both expected and unexpected life shifts. We'll talk about emergency funds, income dips, and how to keep your progress going even when life throws curveballs.

Your job now? Keep showing up. One week at a time. Because the life you're building is already in motion.

This page is left intentionally blank

CHAPTER 14

Staying in the Game – Stay on Track

> *"Discipline isn't about doing it perfectly. It's about showing up—especially when it would be easier to quit."*

☑ 14.1– Story: The Week It Fell Apart

Tasha was doing everything right.

She had mapped out her budget. She was cooking at home. She even celebrated paying off her first credit card two weeks earlier.

But then, one thing hit after another.

Her son's school sent home a surprise fundraiser fee. The electric bill was $48 higher than usual. And her car started making a sound that she knew wasn't free.

Suddenly, she found herself tempted to pull out the very card she had just paid off.

"I felt like I failed. Like the debt was chasing me. I asked myself, what's the point of trying so hard if life keeps knocking me back?"

What Tasha didn't realize was this: **She hadn't failed. She'd just hit a bump in the road.**

Debt elimination isn't a perfect straight line. It's a messy, emotional, real-life journey. And just like with anything that matters—**what keeps you moving isn't perfection, it's the habits you practice when motivation runs out.**

🔍 14.2– What It Means to Stay In the Game

Let's be honest: the beginning of your debt journey is usually the most exciting.

You build a plan, you feel motivated, you start seeing little wins.

But somewhere between the second and sixth month, a sneaky little voice creeps in:

"This is exhausting."
"Is this even working?"
"I miss the freedom to spend."

That voice isn't your enemy. It's your old wiring.
Your brain has been trained to respond to stress, ease, and money in specific ways. Staying in the game means **creating new habits that become your default, even on hard days.**

Let's talk about three essential tools for staying on track: **(1) Weekly check-ins, (2) Crisis management without shame, and (3) Celebrating the right things.**

🔧 14.3– The Weekly Check-In: Discipline Over Drama

The most successful debt eliminators don't rely on motivation—they rely on rhythm.

Every week, they have a 15-minute check-in with themselves.

Not to judge. Not to panic. Just to *notice*.

Here's how to build your rhythm:

🔁 Weekly Ritual: Every Friday or Sunday

- Open this book and look at the tables, the notes you added, the spreadsheets you filled out.
- Ask yourself:
    - What came in (income)?
    - What went out (expenses)?
    - What surprised me?
    - Did I stick to the plan (Snowball or Avalanche)?
    - What's the one small thing I can do better next week?

This is where you build **financial intimacy** with yourself.

It's not about fixing everything in one sitting—it's about not ghosting your money.

Think of it as brushing your financial teeth.
You don't wait for a cavity to floss—you do it because it *prevents problems.*

🧠 14.4– When Setbacks Happen (And They Will)

No debt journey goes perfectly. Life will test your plan. So what do you do when everything falls apart?

🚨 Setback #1: Emergency Strikes

Your fridge dies. Your dog gets sick. Your job cuts hours.

Pause. Breathe. This isn't failure—it's life.

If you've built a small emergency buffer (even $100–$250), now is the time to use it—guilt-free.

If not, make the **next best move**:

- Pause your extra debt payments temporarily.
- Cover the need.
- Adjust the plan without trashing the whole thing.

Resilience doesn't mean nothing ever breaks. It means you *bounce back better.*

🧠 Setback #2: Comparison Kills Progress

Scrolling Instagram while eating rice and beans is brutal.

You see friends with new cars, Caribbean trips, and endless brunches.

But here's what you're not seeing: **the debt they're silently sinking in.**

Don't envy their spending—**envy their silence.**
Because while they're showing off, *you're buying your freedom quietly.*

Repeat this to yourself:

> *"Their life is not my life. Their debt is not my dream."*

🧁 Setback #3: Temptation = Decision Point

You've had a rough week, and suddenly $38 on DoorDash doesn't seem so bad.
That little voice says: *"You've been good. You deserve it."*

You do deserve something.

But what you **deserve more** is to feel proud of yourself next week.

So create a **joy strategy** ahead of time:

- $10/week fun fund
- DIY self-care (bath, walk, book, dance party)
- Text a friend instead of spending

Temptation loses power when you *plan your pleasure with intention.*

🎯 14.5– The Psychology of Small Wins

Your brain needs proof that what you're doing is working.

If your only celebration is at the very end of your debt plan, your motivation will wear out.

So, celebrate often—intentionally, and affordably.

Here's how:

- Paid off a card? Write it on a post-it and stick it where you can see it.
- Hit a 3-month streak? Treat yourself to a no-spend spa night or $5 dessert.
- Saved $100 emergency fund? Dance in your kitchen like you won the lottery.

Celebrating teaches your brain:

"This new behavior brings joy."

That makes it easier to repeat.

▧ Self-Check Exercise: Build Your Mirror Mantra

Purpose: Stay grounded with a visible, emotional anchor.

Steps:

1. Write your current biggest financial win. (It can be small!)
2. Add an encouraging phrase you'll see every day.
3. Stick it on your mirror, fridge, or phone case.

Example Mirror Mantras:

- "I'm not behind. I'm on track."

- "I'm the kind of person who follows through."
- "This plan is working, even if today feels hard."
- "Small steps. Big change. No shame."

✍ Journal Prompt: One Habit I'm Changing

Reflect on this:

- What's one habit I know is holding me back?
- When do I usually fall into it? (Time, emotion, trigger?)
- What could I do differently next time?
- What would change in my life if I let go of that habit?

This is how change sticks—by making the unconscious conscious.

🔄 Rewire Your Story

You might hear this voice in your head:

"I never stick with anything. I always fall off."

Pause.

That's not truth. That's trauma. That's repetition. That's old memory dressed up as fact.

Say this to yourself instead:

> *"I may have stopped before, but I started again. And that's strength."*
> *"Consistency isn't being perfect—it's coming back after you drift."*

Your past doesn't disqualify your progress.

Your comeback is what rewires your brain.

This time, **you're staying in the game.**

💬 Written just for you

"Fall seven times, stand up eight. That's how you win."

📌 Chapter Summary: What You've Conquered

- A personal weekly check-in rhythm
- A system to bounce back from real-life setbacks
- A plan to reward your hard work—without wrecking your budget
- A mirror mantra that reminds you *why* you started
- A habit-changing prompt that brings you closer to your goal

✸ Next Up: Final Chapter – Free, Forever

In the last chapter, we'll talk about how to stay debt-free permanently.

Because freedom isn't fragile when it's built with intention.

You've built strength. Let's make it permanent.

This page is left intentionally blank

CHAPTER 15

The Final Punch

Debt-Free... Now What?

"You've spent years surviving. Now it's time to start designing."

15.1– The Moment It Ends

Jules logged into her account and saw it:

Final payment: $47.19 – Completed.

No fanfare. No confetti. Just a small line of text and a silence so loud it made her heart race.

She stared at the screen for five full minutes.
Then she whispered out loud, as if speaking to the years she spent drowning:

"That's it. I did it."

And then the fear set in.

"What now?"

15.2– Life Without a Balance

Let's pause and acknowledge something big:

You've done something that a lot of people *never* do.

You faced your numbers.

You changed your habits.

You battled emotions.

You stayed in the game.

And now, the balance is gone.

But this is where many people fall into one of two traps:

1. They don't know what to do with the extra money… so they spend it.
2. They're scared of messing up again… so they do nothing.

Neither of those is your future.

You're about to step into your *next chapter*—with clarity, confidence, and choice.

🔧 15.3– Celebrate—But Strategically

Yes, you should celebrate. No, it doesn't need to be expensive.

But it must be **intentional.**

Celebration That Heals:

- Write a letter to your past self: "Thank you for starting."

- Share your story with someone who needs hope.
- Take a "freedom photo" of the moment—print it, frame it.

Why? Because our brains **remember symbolic endings.**

They need emotional closure to create a new identity.

You are no longer "a person in debt."

You are someone who conquered it. That's a shift worth honoring.

🔄 15.4– Reassign the Money

Let's say you were paying $600/month toward debt.

Starting next month, that $600 is now **pure financial power.**
Before you get your hands on our next book about investing, here's a sample roadmap for that new money:

Strategy	**%**	**Amount from $600**
Emergency Fund	30%	$180
Investing / Retirement	25%	$150
Short-Term Goals (vacation, home upgrade)	20%	$120
Fun / Lifestyle	15%	$90
Give / Donate	10%	$60

You can customize the categories—but never let that full amount disappear into random spending.

Money without a purpose always finds a way to vanish.

💡 Real-Life Case Study: Rebuilding After Freedom

Meet ✦Diego, age 38.

He paid off $27,000 in debt over two years. The final payment was a car loan.

Afterward, he felt... lost.

So he followed this three-step plan:

1. Built his 3-month emergency fund in 6 months using freed-up payments.
2. Started investing $200/month into a Roth IRA for the first time.
3. Set a goal: 1 international trip per year—paid in cash.

Now, instead of dread, Diego opens his bank app with **purpose.**
His old $490/month debt payment now funds *peace and possibilities.*

🧠 15.5– New Goals Need New Budgets

Just because you're out of debt doesn't mean the budget is over.

Instead, it evolves.

Your new categories:

- Saving for big purchases
- Retirement investments
- Travel and experiences

- Home improvements
- Giving back
- Passive income building

You're not "cutting back" anymore—you're designing.

Budgeting now becomes a **menu of freedom.**

"What do I want to create with this power?"

✨ 15.6– The Peace of Control

People think money brings peace.

But what actually brings peace is *knowing* what your money is doing.

Debt-free living isn't just about numbers—it's about **mental spaciousness.**

You'll sleep deeper. Breathe easier. Dream wider.

And if something goes wrong again?

You'll know what to do.

Because this time, you have skills. Tools. Experience.

You're not afraid anymore. You're free.

▧ Self-Check: Your After-Debt Vision

Purpose: Anchor your future decisions in your new identity.

Steps:

1. Write down the monthly amount you were sending to debt.
2. List 3 ways you'd love to redirect that amount now.
3. Pick 1 that excites you *and* builds your future.
4. Set up an auto-transfer for it starting next month.

Example:

- Old debt payment: $540
- Redirect: $150 to emergency fund, $200 to IRA, $100 to vacation fund, $90 for fun
- Auto-transfer date: 15th of each month

This becomes your **wealth habit.**

🔄 Rewire Your Story

Old story:

"I've always been bad with money. I'll mess it up again."

New story:

> *"I didn't know then what I know now. But I do now. I've done something powerful. I've proven I can take control. I am trustworthy with money. I can rebuild with wisdom. I have options. And I choose peace."*

Say it out loud, write it down, feel it in your chest.

Let that be the new soundtrack in your head.

💬 **Written just for you**

"Being debt-free isn't the end of your story. It's the blank page where the real story begins."

📌 **Chapter Summary: What You've Conquered**

- **You did it: you closed your last balance. That is historic.**
- Celebrate intentionally—honor your journey, not your pain.
- Redirect your old payments toward your future: freedom, wealth, purpose.
- Your budget still matters—now it's a *freedom blueprint.*
- Peace is found in control, clarity, and consistency.
- Your new identity: financially free, emotionally grounded, powerfully wise.

💬 **Written just for you**

"You don't need to be perfect to win this game. You just need to keep showing up with truth and a plan."

☑ Appendix A: The Last 12 Months Toward Freedom Checklist

"You won't always feel the change day by day—but month by month, your momentum becomes a miracle."

This checklist is your **celebration log** and your **accountability mirror**.

It's not just about numbers—it's about **the choices you've made**, the mindset you've shifted, and the life you've reclaimed, one month at a time.

Each line is a moment to pause, reflect, and write down your win.

📃 Instructions

- Use this checklist **after you've committed to your debt strategy**.
- At the end of each month, take 5–10 minutes to fill it in.
- Don't skip months—even if you had a setback. That's part of your truth too.
- Keep this page visible. Post it on your wall, binder, or fridge.

📅 12-Month Milestone Tracker

Month	Debt Paid This Month	Notes / Challenges	Win I'm Celebrating
Month 1	$________	____________________	____________________

Month 2	$________	____________________	____________________
Month 3	$________	____________________	____________________
Month 4	$________	____________________	____________________
Month 5	$________	____________________	____________________
Month 6	$________	____________________	____________________
Month 7	$________	____________________	____________________
Month 8	$________	____________________	____________________
Month 9	$________	____________________	____________________
Month 10	$________	____________________	____________________
Month 11	$________	____________________	____________________
Month 12	$________	____________________	____________________

🔁 Reflection Questions

At Month 3, 6, 9, and 12—pause and answer:

- *What's changed in how I think about money?*
- *Have I had a financial emergency? How did I handle it?*
- *What financial habit have I stuck with the most?*
- *What new habit do I want to build next?*
- *What would I tell myself if I was starting over right now?*

💬 Motivational Reminders to Post

Tape these quotes where you'll see them often:

✦"Progress isn't perfect—it's just consistent movement in the right direction."
✦"I don't need to feel motivated. I just need to stay committed."
✦"One year of discipline can change my entire life."
✦"Debt doesn't get the last word. I do."

🖼 Appendix B: Motivational Quote Poster Pack

Print. Post. Repeat daily.

"Debt doesn't get the last word. You do."

✨ Print-Friendly Quote Cards

▧ Cut along the lines and tape each quote where it will remind you to stay strong—bathroom mirror, fridge, wallet, or phone case.

"This low balance is not a crisis.
It's proof I'm changing my life."

"I'm not broke—I'm building."

"Every dollar I moved paid down debt.
That money is working for me."

"Progress doesn't always feel good—
but it always pays off."

"One year of discipline can
rewrite your entire financial story."

"I am not my past mistakes.
I am my next smart choice."

"Peace of mind is wealth.
I'm investing in peace."

"Debt doesn't get to own my joy anymore."

"The future me is already proud of today's me."

"Budgeting is not a burden—
it's a rescue mission."

"This is not forever.
This is your freedom season."

"It's okay to rest. Just don't quit."

☑ Appendix C: Your Debt-Free Checklist

A complete summary of everything we've learned in this book—organized by chapter. Use this as your personal tracker. Print and post it somewhere visible.

🧰 HOW TO USE THIS PAGE

✔ Tick the box once you've completed the chapter, understood the case studies, examples, worksheets
🖉 Write the **date you completed** it next to it.
🔁 Return to these as often as needed—they're not one-time tasks.

▧ Chapter Tools / Worksheets — Checklist

☑ **Tool / Worksheet Name**	**Chapter**	**Purpose (reader focused)**	**Date Done**
☐ Face the Debt Wall (Exercise + Worksheet)	1	Gently list every debt so fear shrinks and clarity grows.	____
☐ Wake Up Exercise	2	Spot habits that quietly drain you, so you can choose better.	____
☐ The "Dream vs. Math" Test (Worksheet)	2	Check if your idea fuels freedom—or adds pressure.	____
☐ Personal Reflection Prompt	2	Name what's true for you now and what you want next.	____
☐ Check Your "Invisible" Interest (Self-Check)	3	Reveal hidden interest you're paying and stop the slow leak.	____

☐ CD vs. Credit Card Showdown (Self-Check)	5	Compare apples to apples so your money actually wins.	____
☐ Who's Winning—You or the Bank? (Self-Check)	5	Calculate the score and switch strategies to favor you.	____
☐ Are You Addicted to Financial Chaos? (Self-Check)	6	Notice if stress spending is running the show and reset.	____
☐ Picture Your Debt-Free Paycheck (Self-Check)	6	See how free your income can feel—and plan for it.	____
☐ Budget Readiness Score (Self-Check)	7	Check if your budget can handle real life—then tighten gently.	____
☐ Fixed vs. Flexible Spending Sort (Self-Check)	7	Separate must-pays from choices to find easy wins.	____
☐ My Current Debt Snapshot (Worksheet)	9	Capture all balances and rates in one place to start your game plan.	____
☐ What I Really Have Left Each Month (Cash Flow Worksheet)	9	Know your real leftover so you can attack debt on purpose.	____
☐ Debt Timeline Vision (Self-Check)	9	Map the next 12 months to turn progress into momentum.	____
☐ SMART Goal Builder (Self-Check)	10	Build specific, measurable goals before choosing strategy.	____
☐ My Monthly Action Plan (Self-Check)	13	Turn your chosen strategy into weekly/monthly actions.	____
☐ Build Your Mirror Mantra (Self-Check)	14	Anchor new habits with affirmations during setbacks.	____
☐ Your After-Debt Vision (Self-Check)	15	Redirect freed-up money toward peace, wealth, and purpose.	____

☐ Your First 90 Days Debt-Free (Worksheet)	15	Practical steps to build habits once payments end.	____

🧠 Quizzes — Checklist

☑ Quiz Title	Chapter	Purpose (reader focused)	Date Done
☐ Building a Strong Financial Foundation	1	Test your basics—budgeting, DTI, financial health, income, expenses.	____
☐ Navigating the Debt Landscape (Quiz 2)	3	Check your grasp of debt types, interest, and smart decision rules.	____

💬 Reminder

"Debt freedom is a journey, not a race. These tools are here to guide—not judge. Come back to them, update them, reuse them. They're yours."

✸ Final Take – Parting Words From the Author

I know what it feels like to wake up and feel like money controls everything.

What you eat. What you say yes to. What you say no to.

How you sleep at night—or don't.

The stress of choosing between peace and bills.

The silent guilt of feeling "behind," even when you've been doing your best with what you were given.

If that's you, I need you to know something right now:

You are not behind. You are starting. And that's the most powerful place to be.

Debt doesn't make you weak.

Living paycheck to paycheck doesn't mean you failed.

Not knowing how to budget or use credit isn't a flaw—it's a gap in education.

And this book—this journey—has been about filling that gap.

You've done something most people don't.

You stayed with it. You faced hard truths. You asked yourself real questions.

And whether your balance is $3,000 or $330,000, you now have something you didn't before:

Power. Clarity. Courage.

And let me tell you what happens when someone like you—someone brave enough to keep reading, to keep showing up—gains power, clarity, and courage:

They change their life.

They change their family's life.

They change what the next generation thinks is "normal."

If you've ever doubted that you could be the one to break the cycle—of financial stress, confusion, fear—I hope this book helped you see the truth:

You are already breaking it.

Every worksheet you filled, every exercise you tried, every moment you paused to reflect—that's you shifting gears. That's you reprogramming your financial identity.

So as you move forward, I leave you with this:

- Keep tracking, even when it's boring.
- Keep budgeting, even when you mess up one month.
- Keep attacking your plan, even if it takes longer than expected.
- Keep protecting your peace, even when the world tells you to spend it all.
- Keep rewriting the story, even when your past tries to speak louder than your future.

And remember: **your money is not just about money.**

It's about freedom.

It's about choosing rest over stress.

It's about no longer asking permission to live your life.

You didn't need to be perfect to get here.

You just needed to be willing.

And you were.

So go forward.

Dream bigger.

And when doubt tries to whisper in your ear again, say this out loud:

"I am not broke. I am building."

"I am not behind. I am just getting started."

With all my heart,

– Regine

"One day you'll look back and realize this was the moment you stopped surviving and started living."

rg.
REGINE GODEFROY
AUTHOR

About the Author

Regine Godefroy is an entrepreneur, business coach, and author committed to helping everyday people take control of their money and build lasting freedom. With more than 30 years of real-world experience, she has guided individuals, families, and small business owners in breaking free from debt, boosting credit, and creating sustainable financial plans.

She is the creator of the *Money Made Simple Series*, designed to walk readers step by step from budgeting and saving (***Start With This***), to debt elimination (***Get Out of Debt Fast***), and onward to credit mastery and investing.

Through her books, coaching, and online courses, Regine empowers readers to move from financial stress to financial strength—showing that no matter where you start, freedom is possible.

rg.
REGINE GODEFROY
AUTHOR

Continue Your Journey With Shopunlocked

www.shopunlocked.com

✔ **Budget & Savings Coaching**

— build a money plan that works

✔ **Debt Elimination Coaching**

— create your personal debt-free roadmap

✔ **Credit Boost Coaching**

— raise your score and unlock new opportunities

✔ **Amazon Seller Courses**

— launch and grow your online business

✔ **Amazon FBM Support**

— guidance to scale your store successfully

Enjoyed This Book?

If *Get Out of Debt Fast* helped you, would you take a minute to share your thoughts?

Your honest review on Amazon means more than you think:

- It helps other readers discover the book.
- It supports independent authors like me.
- It inspires me to keep creating tools and resources for your financial journey.

👉 **Scan this QR Code & leave your review on Amazon today — and help someone else start their debt-free journey!**

Thank you for being part of this mission.

— Regine

Made in the USA
Monee, IL
04 November 2026

67387599R00144